Surf the waves of opportunity

SURF THE WAVES OF OPPORTUNITY

LEAD YOUR BUSINESS
TO OPERATIONAL EXCELLENCE
WITH FIVE THINGS DONE RIGHT

Dietrich (Dieter) Legat

The German National Library (German: *Deutsche Nationalbibliothek* or DNB) is the central archival library and national bibliographic center for the Federal Republic of Germany.
Details of bibliographic data: *http://dnb.dnb.de*

Surf the Waves of Opportunity
Lead your business to operational excellence with five things done right
Version 2.0, 2017

© 2017 Dietrich Legat

Illustrations: Dietrich Legat
Figure 1.1: Surfer, Ross Clarke Jones, rides a giant wave while surfing at Waimea Bay during Quiksilver Eddie Aikau Big Wave surfing contest in Hawaii.
Licensed from www.dreamstime.com

Production and publisher: BoD – Books on Demand, Norderstedt, Germany

ISBN: 978-3-7431-6589-2

Hardcover version (illustrations in color) ISBN: 978-3-7392-1010-0

Elevator pitch

Are you managing a business or a business unit or is your goal to achieve such positions? Then this book is for you. It summarizes what I have learned about operational leadership over more than 50 years as a business manager and top management consultant[1]:

Operational leadership determines company success

Top management's job is to spot the waves of opportunity and lead the company in riding them. Visionary and strategic thinking is required to spot waves. Operational leadership leads the company in riding them. It's like surfing big waves. To spot one is important, but success lies in riding it without falling off the surfboard.

Lead a far reaching living system, not just a moneymaking machine

Your business is a living creature, a self-organizing and self-creating system. It comprises every element that supports us in or hinders us from achieving our goals. It is much more than the company. All of the elements in the entire business ecosystem are part of the whole system.

For success in operational leadership, you must do five things right

To lead this living organism, do five things right, in a never-ending cycle of agile leadership:

- One: Set the right operational goals to establish the line on which you want to surf your wave. You only need one: contribution margin.
- Two: Plan. Build your surfboard. Design the right plan: Focus it on resolving constraints. Write it down on one single page.
- Three: Execute. Surf your wave. Follow the goal to deliver the obligations outlined in your operational plan.

---

[1] Working for AEG-Telefunken, Honeywell and Hewlett Packard, and since 2001 as consultant to top managers from start-ups to international concerns.

- Four: Check. Review progress against your goal and execution of your operational plan. Go back to planning if the operational plan needs to be adjusted.
- Five: Add the value required from operational leaders. Lead your Plan-Execute-Check cycle to spin faster than your competitors. Institutionalize the culture of operational excellence.

Operational leadership is all about surfing monster waves of opportunity. It strains us to our limits. Yet it is the most fascinating and rewarding task in business management. You will likely become addicted, as I did.

Shall we go? – Great, let's go surfing.

Dieter Legat. Geneva (Switzerland), January 2016

PS: You are welcome to use my charts free of charge for your own work and presentations. Please find the charts for download at http://www.book-agile-operational-leadership.com

Thank you for helping me to write this book

Thank you, Bill[2], for your patience and generous advice in so many aspects of TOC and how it should be applied correctly. Your comments and guidance were of extreme value for me and clarified several key aspects covered in this book.

Thank you, Soin[3], for coaching me in the practices of total quality management. You taught me how to diagnose levels of operational maturity and design an improvement plan that leads a business to outstanding operational results. Special thanks for teaching me to not push ropes.

Thank you, Branka[4], for teaching me so much in the domain of emotional decision making. Every time we meet you open another door for me, giving me deeper insight into this fascinating field.

Thank you, Gabriel[5], for taking the time in the most busy time of the business year, to review my manuscript in detail and for submitting agile business leadership to the tough test of reality in business.

Thank you, Bill[6], for your patience and for introducing me to TOC, for arranging a memorable one-day meeting with Eliyahu Goldratt, for your ever-present down to earth advice from the point of view of a successful top manager and for your valuable comments to the manuscript of this book.

Thank you, Cary[7], for your advice in creating this book. Your insight and guidance relative the world of creating books and your patient help as copy-editor were very, very, valuable to me.

And thank you, Bernadette, my dear wife, for your support in all those years and for being such an incredibly strong role model for how to cope with seemingly insurmountable constraints.

---

[2] William Dettmer. Senior Partner of Goals System International. Author of the leading book on TOC logics, "The logical thinking process".

[3] Sarv Singh Soin. Experienced leader of supply chain systems, leader in the HP Quality/Operational excellence project. Recent book "Winning with operational excellence"

[4] Branka Zei-Pollermann, renowned expert in emotional decision making, founder of Vox Institute, Geneva (Switzerland)

[5] Gabriel Migy, Head of strategic planning, BOBST Group

[6] William A. Woehr. Retired HP sales executive. Co-author of the book "Unblock the power of your sales force!"

[7] Cary Sherburne. World leading expert in printing technology and guardian angel of business writers. http://www.sherburneassociates.com/

Dietrich (Dieter) Legat

Born 1938 in Graz (Austria), Dieter is married, with two daughters and four grandchildren. He is an avid biker, skier and photographer and lives in Geneva, Switzerland.

Dieter studied petroleum engineering at the University of Leoben, Austria and then continued as Assistant at the Institute of Mathematics. In that role he worked with computers for the first time – which was the beginning of his career in computer business. There, starting in 1964, he first worked for AEG-Telefunken (then a GE OEM) and then joined Honeywell (Computer Operations Europe). In 1974 he moved to Hewlett Packard. There, he enjoyed a career in sales management and quality management, where he guided the European computer business unit to win the HP President's Quality Award, awarded by the late Lew Platt, then HP President and CEO.

His last assignment before retiring from HP was operational planning manager for HP's global accounts business.

During his time at HP, as part of his job, he consulted with many companies, sharing HP practices in operational leadership.

After retiring from HP in 2001 Dieter began a second career as top management consultant, specializing in operational leadership. In this role, he has served top management of more than 30 companies from small start-ups to large multinational corporations in information technology, finance, machine engineering, and pharmaceuticals.

For several years, Dieter taught operational leadership in a FIBAA[8] certified postgraduate course for business managers, at the University of Graz, Austria.

In 2002 with his friend and long time HP colleague Bill Woehr he wrote the book Unblock the power of your sales force!, which introduces the theory of constraints for the domain of sales leadership. The book was also published in German and Japanese.

---

[8] Foundation for interational business administration accreditation

Content

Elevator pitch 1
Chapter 1: Surf the waves of opportunity 11
    The management value chain 12
    Operational excellence 16
Chapter 2: Five right 19
    Five tasks done right 20
    Agile operational leadership 21
Chapter 3: Systems view required 25
    One element of the entire business ecosystem 26
    One function can constrain the whole 28
    A living creature 31
    Not just a money making machine 32
Chapter 4: Right goals 33
    The meaning of "goal" 34
    Goals in the management value chain 35
    One single operational business goal: sufficient income 38
    Operational business goals for company business units 41
    Operational business goals with the right content 43
    Operational goals right for execution 45
Chapter 5: Avoid the traps of intuition 49
    System 1 and System 2 50
    Two deadly traps of intuition to avoid 50
    Trap Number 1: WYSIATI - What you see is all there is 51
    Trap Number 2: Jumping to conclusions 52
Chapter 6: Right operational plans 55
    Two purposes for operational plans 56
    Causal trees from goal to action 57
    One-page operational plans 58
    Limitations of top-down planning 61
    Autonomous operational plans for company business units 64
    Operationalize the elements of operational plans 67
Chapter 7: Critical success factors 71
    CSFs: non-negotiable conditions for the operational goal 72
    Firm on strategic level. Flexible for operational leadership 72
    Anywhere within the entire business ecosystem 73
    Six rules for identifying the right critical success factors (CSFs) 75

Worksheet and operational plan 76
Chapter 8: Competitors' plans 79
　　Our competitors – systems view 80
　　Understanding competitors' performance 82
　　Customer's view of your competitors... 83
　　Competitor's operational leadership 84
　　Three rules for understanding competitors' plans 88
　　Worksheet and operational plan 89
Chapter 9: Necessary conditions 93
　　MUST ACHIEVE performance levels of the business system 94
　　Four rules for setting right NCs 95
　　Worksheet and operational plan 98
Chapter 10: Obstacles 101
　　Obstacle, defined 102
　　Physical obstacles 103
　　Emotional obstacles 103
　　Three rules for defining right obstacles 106
　　Worksheet and operational plan 107
Chapter 11: Commitments 111
　　Operational commitments: Promises for new system states 112
　　Four rules for establishing right commitments 113
　　Worksheet and operational plan 116
Chapter 12: All obligations confirmed 119
Chapter 13: Right execution 121
　　The entire operational team on one surfboard 122
　　1. Focus attention on the operational business goal 122
　　2. Track progress toward necessary conditions 124
　　3. Flawlessly deliver against obligations 126
Chapter 14: Right check 129
　　Deep reviews – tuned to the level of operational performance 130
　　Improving the management of obligations 134
　　Refining the operational plan 135
　　Finding constraints in the business system 136
　　Plan to resolve the constraint 140
Chapter 15: Right operational leadership 143
　　Leading our PEC cycles: Four leadership events 144
　　Leading key event No.1: The operational planning workshop 145
　　Leading key event No.2: Meetings 154
　　Leading key event No. 3: Quick Review 155

    Leading key event No.4: Deep review 157
    Leading competence in PEC cycles 160
    Leading a culture of operational excellence 166
    Breakthrough goals culture 168
    Team culture 169
    Agile culture 171
    Managers are not the constraint 172
    Positive emotions culture 176
Chapter 16: Now, it's your turn 181
Chapter 17: The DELTA T Cockpit 183
    The tool to support and simplify operational leadership 185
    Scalable, flexible, worldwide access 187
Thank you for teaching me 189
Abbreviations 191
Books 193
Index 197

Chapter 1: Surf the waves of opportunity

Figure 1.1 Top management's job is twofold
Vision and strategy: To see the waves of opportunity coming.
Operational leadership: To lead the company to ride them. Better than competition.

Dick Hackborn[9], who led HP into the printer business, defined a business leader's job in short and clear terms: "To see the waves of opportunity and lead the company to ride them".

As business leaders we need vision to see coming waves of opportunity and strategy to select the best position on these waves. However, vision and strategy alone are not enough. We must also lead the company or the business unit to ride the wave. That is the role of operational leadership.

In this chapter we position operational leadership where it deserves to be: as the prime driver for consistent lasting business success. It is an element in the management value chain in its own right. Its purpose is to lead our business to achieve its to-date goals consistently.

---

[9] Hackborn, Richard A., former HP executive

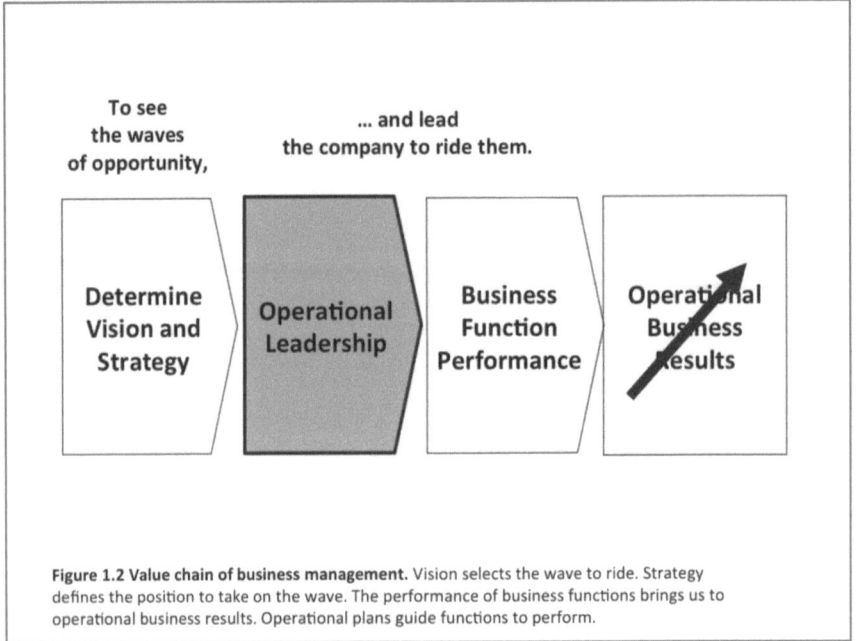

Figure 1.2 Value chain of business management. Vision selects the wave to ride. Strategy defines the position to take on the wave. The performance of business functions brings us to operational business results. Operational plans guide functions to perform.

The management value chain

Viewed as value chain, business management consists of four elements: determine vision and strategy, operational leadership, business function performance and operational business results. Generations of managers have learned to view this chain from start to end: We start with vision and strategy. From there on we subordinate everything else in the management value chain to these two.

Let's now regard this value chain, as we would do with a manufacturing process, starting at the end and going upstream from there:

- Operational business results are the purpose, the end result of business leadership,
- Going upstream from there, we subordinate every link in the chain to that purpose, each serving the next in chain.

First, the operational business results: The purpose

All of the efforts of a business have one - and only one - purpose: to achieve its operational business goals. The degree to which these goals are achieved is the level of "operational excellence". Business processes, operational leadership, strategy and vision are but tools to achieve that purpose.

Second, business functions: Deliver business results meeting the operational goals

Each function's performance is subordinated to the business goals. Their added value is to achieve or perform at the performance goal levels required for the entire business to achieve its goal. Activities not aimed at operational business goals are wasted effort and diminish effectiveness and efficiency.

Third, operational leadership: Lead functions deliver their contribution

Operational leadership sets functions' performance goals, subordinated to the business goals and leads the functions to deliver against these.

Operational plans – the backbone of operational leadership

Operational plans are the backbone for this task. They comprise functions' performance goals and the actions for how to achieve these.

They are the surfboards that enable us to surf our wave. Every surfing beach and every wave are different, so we build a special one for each area and wave. In addition, we check and adjust our surfboard continuously, adapting it to the constantly changing conditions of our wave.

Our success in surfing is highly dependent on how adequate our surfboard is for a specific wave.

Operational leadership creates company success

The value chain view shows that operational leadership – not vision or strategy – creates a company's success. This is where our thinking is brutally tested against reality, where all the great models and concepts are put to the test.

Seldom acknowledged and very difficult

Operational leadership is seldom acknowledged as a separate discipline of management, as John P. Kotter, renowned expert on leadership and change points out:[10]

> *Although traditional hierarchies and managerial processes (the components of a company's operating system) can meet the daily demands of running an enterprise, they are rarely equipped to quickly identify important hazards, formulate creative initiatives, and implement them.*
>
> *"… Need an additional element to address the challenges produced by mounting complexity and rapid change. … a second operating system, devoted to the design and implementation of strategy, that uses an agile, networklike structure and a very different set of processes. The new operating system continually assesses the business, the industry, and the organization, and reacts with greater agility, speed, and creativity than the existing one. …. It actually makes enterprises easier to run and accelerates strategic change. This is not an "either or" idea. It's "both and."*

Not only is operational leadership often not recognized as required, it is also much more difficult than creating vision and writing strategy, and the risk of failure is high:

> *One disturbing reality that our research has turned up is a major fault line at the front end of innovation. Booz & Company's most recent Global Innovation 1000 study revealed that just 43% of senior innovation executives and chief technology officers at nearly 700 companies believe their organizations are highly effective at generating new ideas, and only 36% believe they are highly effective at converting ideas to product development projects. Still fewer – one-quarter of respondents – indicate that their organizations are highly effective at both.[11]*

---

[10] Kotter, John P.: Accelerate! Harvard Business Review. Nov.2012.

[11] 2014 Global Innovation Study, INSEAD

Chapter 1: Surf the waves of opportunity

Fourth, vision and strategy: Provide information for operational planning

Vision and strategy need to provide information for operational planning. There are three categories of information required by operational plans:

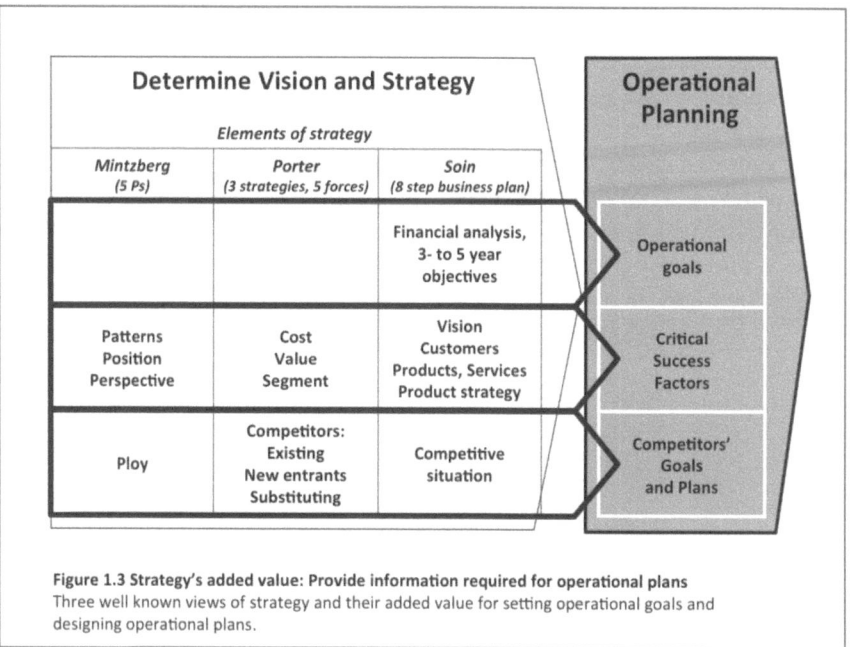

Figure 1.3 Strategy's added value: Provide information required for operational plans
Three well known views of strategy and their added value for setting operational goals and designing operational plans.

- Information for setting the operational goal: As a basis for setting the right operational goal a longer range (2-3 years) financial plan is required. It must take into account seasonality, product rollover and other aspects, which shape the goals over time.
- Information for determining the critical success factors: These are the elements upon which the operational plan must focus in order to lead functions to the required performance. For these, vision needs to tell us about new waves and what they will be like. Strategy needs to provide information on customers (segments, position, trends), products and services (road maps, value added) encompassed by the new wave.
- Information for understanding competitors' plans: These elements of our operational plan determine how we will cope with our competitors. For this we need strategy to tell us whom we must expect as competitors, how they will differ from us and which goals and plans we should expect from them.

15

Figure 1-3 shows how elements of strategy, as defined by three leading authorities - Henry Mintzberg[12] ("5Ps"), Michael E. Porter[13] (3 generic strategies) and Soin Singh[14] (9 step business plan) - relate to elements of operational plans.

Operational excellence

The purpose of operational leadership is to achieve operational excellence of the company.
- For methods experts, operational excellence means to make business functions deliver key performance metrics by using a toolbox of methods.[15]
- For operational leaders, operational excellence has a different meaning. It is a state of business performance, which is reached, when our business consistently achieves its "to date" operational goals.

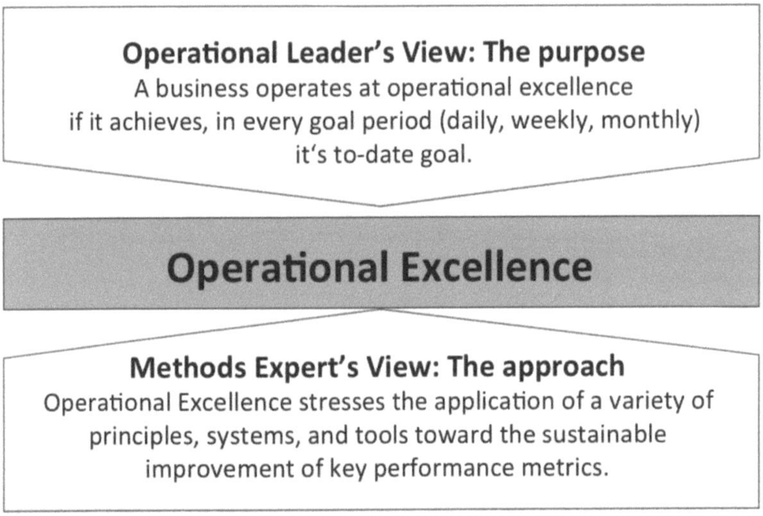

Operational Leader's View: The purpose
A business operates at operational excellence if it achieves, in every goal period (daily, weekly, monthly) it's to-date goal.

Operational Excellence

Methods Expert's View: The approach
Operational Excellence stresses the application of a variety of principles, systems, and tools toward the sustainable improvement of key performance metrics.

Figure 1.4 Operational excellence - Two views
Leader's view recognizes operational excellence from the point of view of the outcome.
Methods expert's view stresses methodologies.

---

[12] http://www.ifm.eng.cam.ac.uk/research/dstools/mintzbergs-5-ps-for-strategy/

[13] https://en.wikipedia.org/wiki/Porter's_generic_strategies

[14] Soin, Sarv Singh: Total quality essentials. Updated edition. Mc Graw Hill, New York. 1992. P.51 ff

[15] http://en.wikipedia.org/wiki/Operational_excellence

At first glance this definition makes it seem like we are putting too much emphasis on achieving short-term goals (at the expense of longer term results). This is only the case when our strategy did not define longer-term goals as the framework for short-term - for instance annual - goals. When the strategy defines longer-term goals as the framework for short-term goals, the shorter-term annual goals are subordinated to longer-term goals.

"To date" performance is more realistic than performance by a shorter measurement interval, like a month or a week, as the cumulating results smoothens out short-term variations in results.

Hewlett Packard, showcase of operational excellence[16]

What does operational excellence look like? HP is a good example. Readers know this company for its market leading products in electronic test and measurement, computers and printers. The company's outstanding historical results in revenue and profit are less known. HP consistently delivered growth in revenue and earnings, year after year, to a large degree self-financed.

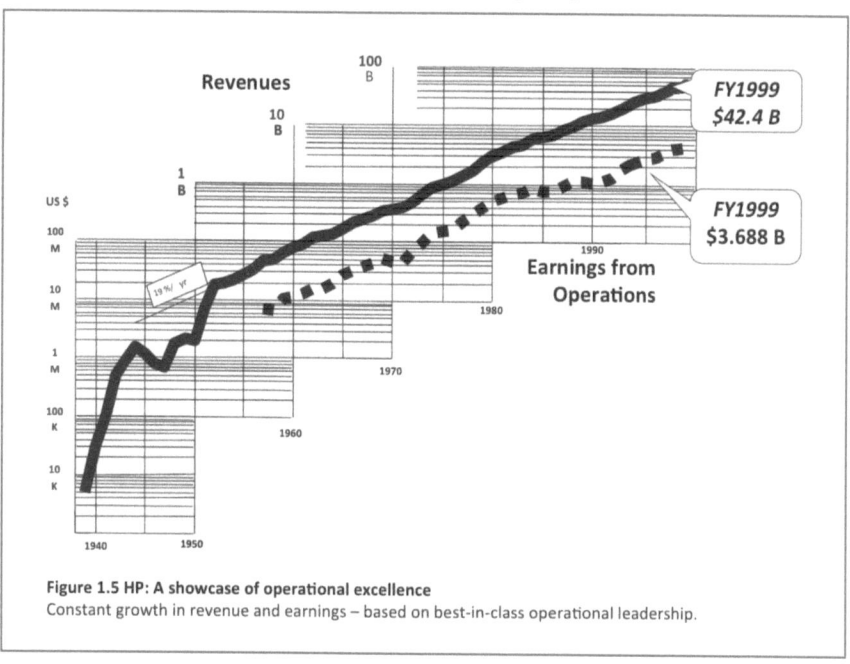

Figure 1.5 HP: A showcase of operational excellence
Constant growth in revenue and earnings – based on best-in-class operational leadership.

---

[16] Having worked for HP for 27 years of course I have recognized many of its management practices as leading to the operational excellence the company achieved. Dieter Legat

One perspective is that these were the easy high times of booming markets in electronics. They were not. Many companies skyrocketed for a short time and then disappeared. Take the computer business for example. Where are its heroes of yesterday? RCA? GE? Honeywell? Bull? Data General? Wang? Control Data? ICL? Ferranti? Cray? Digital Equipment? Burroughs? Tandem? SUN? Nixdorf? Siemens? Compaq?

Compared to these shooting stars HP results never were spectacular. But, in the longer run, HP outperformed them. HP managers were masters of leading the company to and keeping it at operational excellence.

Chapter 2: Five right

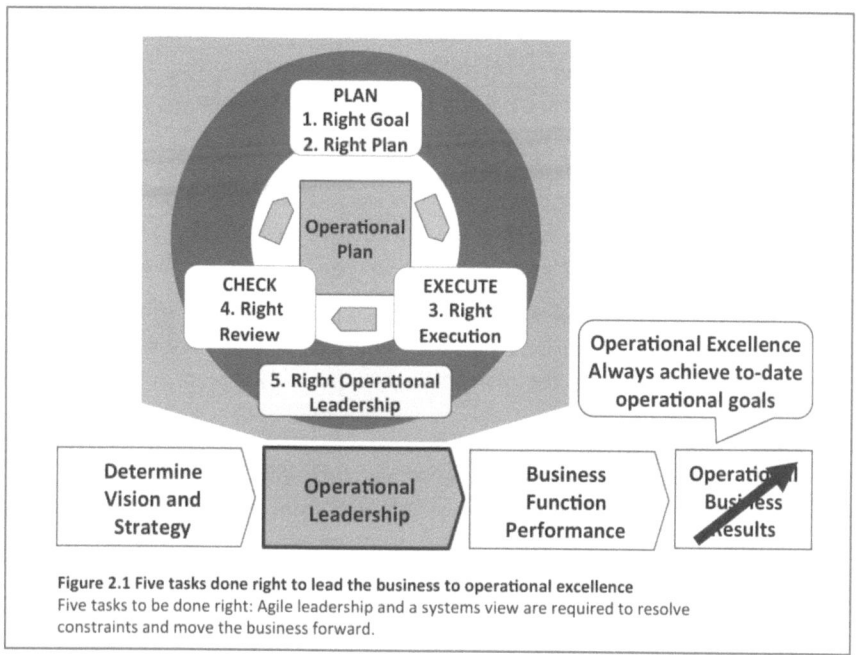

Figure 2.1 Five tasks done right to lead the business to operational excellence
Five tasks to be done right: Agile leadership and a systems view are required to resolve constraints and move the business forward.

To lead your business to or at operational excellence in these times of incessant and rapid change you must do five tasks right:
- Set the right goals,
- Design the right operational plans,
- Execute them right,
- Check your plans for adjustment and improvement and
- Have the right operational leadership in place.

These tasks must be led with an agile approach: in a never-ending cycle of Plan-Execute-Check, the PEC cycle.

Such are the principles of an extremely flexible, continuously adjusting approach to leadership – as required for surfing the waves of opportunity.

Five tasks done right

Operational leadership consists of five tasks. If done right and performed in a never-ending agile cycle, the business will reach operational excellence.

Task One: Set the right operational goals

The fundamental plank of operational excellence is setting the right operational goals for the business, its units, functions and people.

Task Two: Design the right operational plan

The right operational plan does not just give everyone something to do. Not everyone needs goals, not everything needs to be cascaded down from the top. It just contains the vital few things to be done to bring us to our goal. William A. (Bill) Woehr

This is the master plan. It defines, who will do what to bring the business to the goals. It is the surfboard, perfectly adjusted to the wave we want to ride. People with obligations in the plan form the operational team.

Task Three: Right execution

We have built our surfboard. Now, we surf. This is the toughest part of operational leadership. It requires our full attention, constant focus and rapid, precise execution of even the slightest movement. Not for one moment can you take your eyes off the goal and relax in delivering against obligations.

"Quick reviews" are the key event of executing operational plans. In this review operational teams check progress in executing the plan's obligations.

Task Four: Right check

Everything changes always. Within our companies, functions, people, organizations and performance levels change. Beyond that, customers change, as do politics, competitors, suppliers and partners. If we allow it to remain static the operational plan will be soon not right anymore. Check it (your surfboard) regularly and adjust it as needed.

The "deep review" is the key event to check whether the plan is still right. Item by item, the operational team critically reviews the plan and eventually decides whether and how to adjust it.

Task Five: Right operational leadership

The added value of operational leaders is twofold: To have each step of the PEC (plan, lead, check) cycle done right and to develop the competence of the operational teams.

Agile operational leadership

Agile software development

When designing a new software function you often do not and even cannot know in advance the full impact for the user in the widely distributed and networked IT systems which companies have today. The user cannot verbalize the impact, unless he has tried the software in practice.

To cope, software developers developed the agile approach. Instead of starting with a complete software specification they collect a list of user requirements (the backlog). From it they choose the few most valuable ones and deliver these in a fast "sprint".

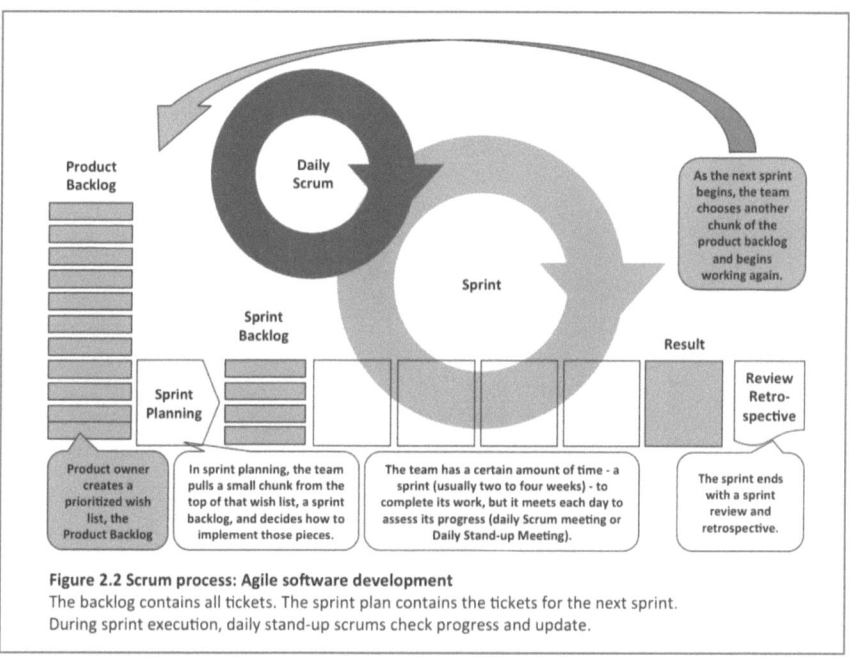

Figure 2.2 Scrum process: Agile software development
The backlog contains all tickets. The sprint plan contains the tickets for the next sprint. During sprint execution, daily stand-up scrums check progress and update.

Two key events drive the progress. In the "daily stand-up meeting" (also called daily scrum meeting) the sprint team assesses progress in the sprint. In the "sprint retrospective" the team checks the sprint result with the user/customer, plans the next sprint and seeks ways to improve the approach.

This approach has proven to be much more realistic, faster and more cost effective than the traditional process of first specifying the entire product and then building the program in its entirety.

The agile approach must not be confused with sloppy design, which may lead to "charging your customer for the privilege of paying for your learning curve"[17]. It is important to note that each item at the end of a sprint must be fully completed and tested. This leaves no room for sloppiness.

---

[17] Comment from H. William Dettmer

Agile operational sprints

A general assumption behind much of the planning literature is that the process itself is not dynamic... Well, all of this is fiction.[18] *If empirical research has taught us anything at all ... it is that the process is a fundamentally dynamic one, corresponding to the dynamic conditions that drive it.*

Operational leaders face challenges similar to those in software development.

The wave being ridden changes continuously. The cycle of Plan-Execute-Check (PEC) is the cycle of agile leadership. One turn in the cycle is equivalent to one operational sprint. The operational plan is the sprint backlog for the next period, for example quarter year.

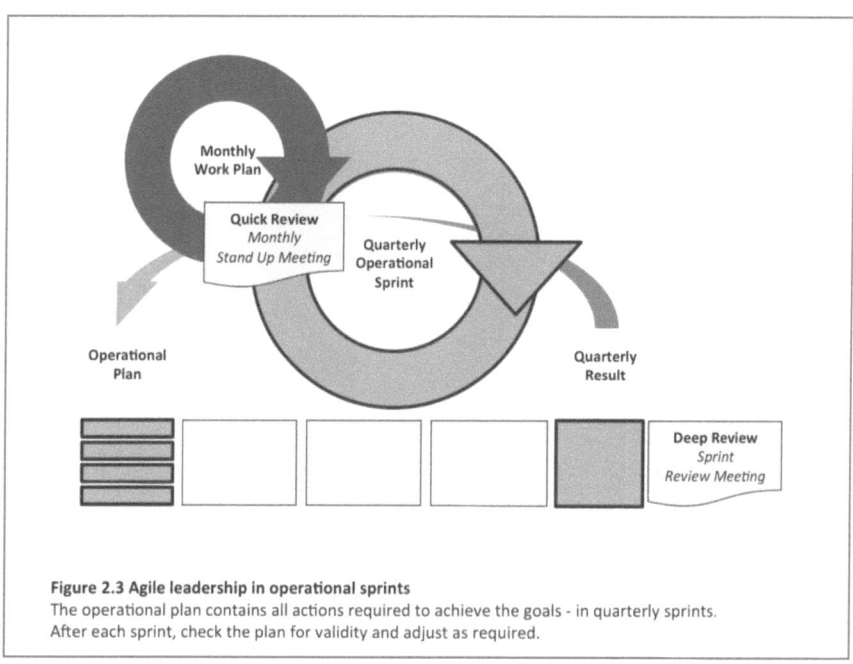

Figure 2.3 Agile leadership in operational sprints
The operational plan contains all actions required to achieve the goals - in quarterly sprints. After each sprint, check the plan for validity and adjust as required.

---

[18] Mintzberg, Henry: The Rise and Fall of Strategic Planning. Simon and Schuster, 1994. P.241

As in software development there are two key events required to execute operational sprints: the "quick review", the term used in operational leadership for stand-up meetings, and the "deep review", equivalent to the operational sprint review meeting.

Cyclical approaches are well known in management. Examples are: Shewhart's PDC cycle, Deming's PDCA cycle, Six Sigma's DMAIC Cycle, Goldratt's POOGI cycle, and John Boyd's OODA loop.

The PEC cycle differs from these in that its main focus is not on processes, but on operational plans and the tasks required to design, execute and adjust them for the purpose of leading the business to or at operational excellence.

Chapter 3: Systems view required

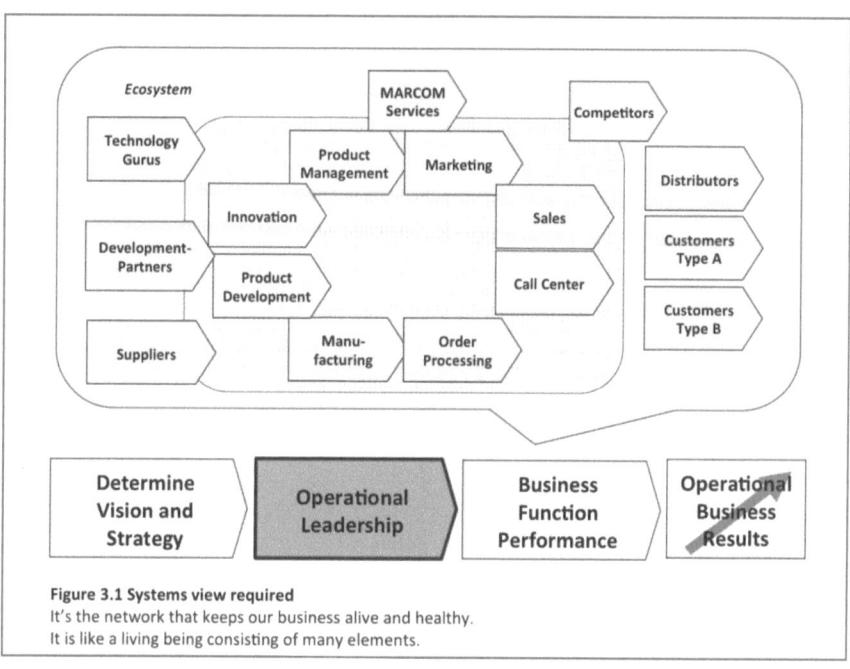

Figure 3.1 Systems view required
It's the network that keeps our business alive and healthy.
It is like a living being consisting of many elements.

In this new world of rapidly changing networked companies business leaders must recognize that their view of what they lead needs to change. They are not just leading organizations, hierarchies, business units or employees. Rather, they lead a value-adding network, goal determined, self-organizing and social – in other words: their business system.[19]

The systems view recognizes the company as one element in its business ecosystem. Within that it is a self-organizing and self-creating living being gifted with both physical and social features, where one function can constrain the whole.

---

[19] Hans-Peter Liebmann, Professor em. of Marketing & Sales, University of Graz (Austria).

One element of the entire business ecosystem

The business system contains all functions that help it to or hinder it from reaching its goals. Therefore it includes not only its internal functions, but also all other elements or functions in its entire business ecosystem.

A business ecosystem is ... an economic community supported by a foundation of interacting organizations and individuals—the organisms of the business world. The economic community produces goods and services of value to customers, who are themselves members of the ecosystem. The member organisms also include suppliers, lead producers, competitors, and other stakeholders. James F. Moore[20]

Boeing, for example, builds its 787 Dreamliner aircraft within a far-reaching business ecosystem. Its success is dependent on many elements, many of which are not located inside Boeing. Companies in Canada, Australia, Japan, Korea and Europe are part of the Boeing business ecosystem.

Including the business ecosystem in your view gives you a better opportunity to design the right plans. Critical success factors may exist both internally and externally. Operational projects define temporary networks of functions from anywhere in the ecosystem. Obstacles may appear in any element. When searching for root cause constraints, it is important to check every single function for causal relationships explaining an undesired situation.

---

[20] https://en.wikipedia.org/wiki/Business_ecosystem

Chapter 3: Systems view required

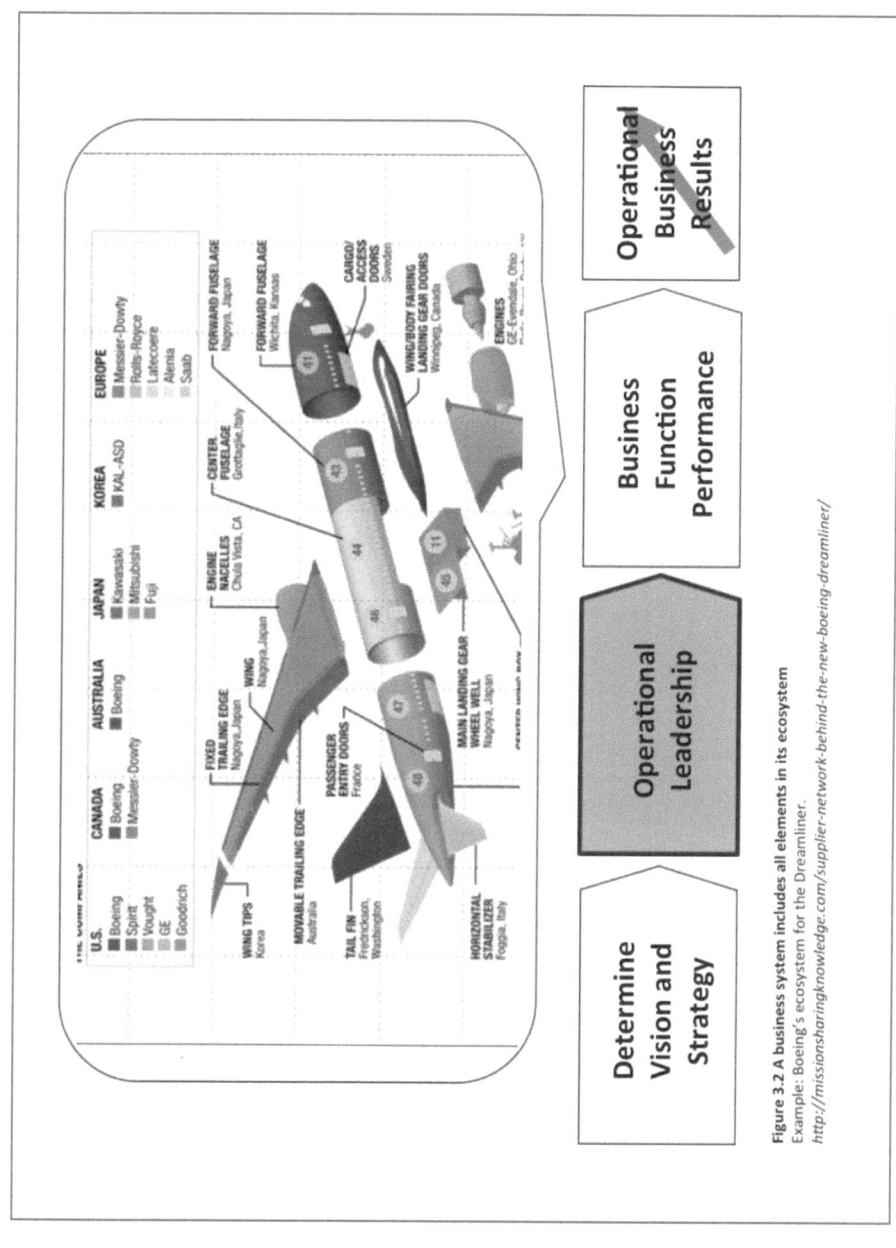

Figure 3.2 A business system includes all elements in its ecosystem
Example: Boeing's ecosystem for the Dreamliner.
http://missionsharingknowledge.com/supplier-network-behind-the-new-boeing-dreamliner/

One function can constrain the whole

Sometimes it seems that we are doing everything right. Contribution margin grows. But then almost overnight growth comes to a halt. BANG!

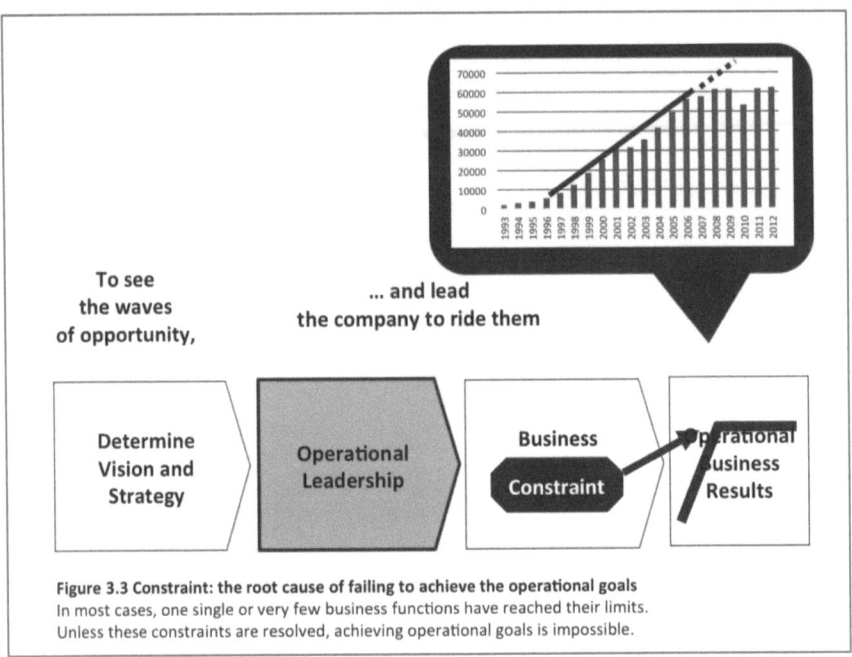

Figure 3.3 Constraint: the root cause of failing to achieve the operational goals
In most cases, one single or very few business functions have reached their limits. Unless these constraints are resolved, achieving operational goals is impossible.

Sales managers might claim that the new products cannot be sold – that they are not what the customer wants and are too expensive. Product managers might accuse sales managers and sales people of incompetence. Manufacturing managers might bring up a strike in their plant in New Hampshire. Finance managers might explain the devastating impact of the recent change in currency policy of the government. What has happened?

Constraint, defined

By taking a systems view, you can better understand that the business has hit a constraint: one or a few of the business system's functions cannot cope with the workload. They are a choke point for the system and constrain the entire system. They are the root cause of the undesired effect of the business system not reaching its operational business goal.

Constraint: the root cause in a network of symptoms

To deliver value to customers, the business system organizes its functions to work in a networked flow. All efforts aim to create value for the customer. Events in one function trigger positive or negative consequences in others.

In Switzerland, for instance, people use multi-lingual keyboards like German/French or German/Italian. A company may have the best sales force, the best performing products, the best level of service – if their keyboards are not meeting the multi-lingual requirements success will be limited.

When one function becomes a constraint it triggers consequences in other functions, which can then limit our results. Such consequences are symptoms, not the root cause of the problem.

Mid year business review. Our sales results were in trouble. Forecast did not look better. Management meeting. Heated discussion. Then, decision: set a "challenge goal" for the sales force and make the commission scheme more aggressive for the rest of the year.

Three months later.... no improvement in sales results and forecast. We had addressed a symptom – not the constraint.

This root cause must be found and resolved. Just fixing symptoms is both ineffective and a waste of company energy.

Chapter 3: Systems view required

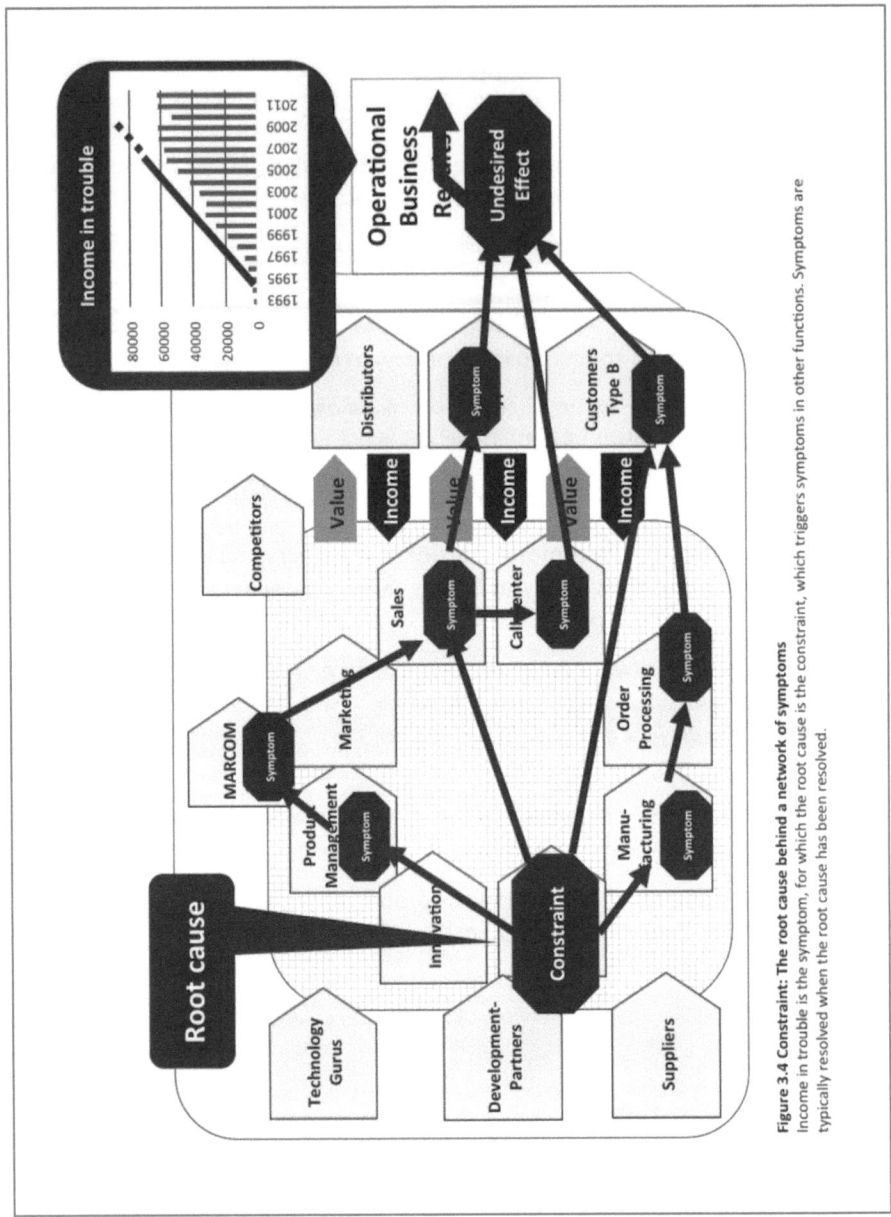

Figure 3.4 Constraint: The root cause behind a network of symptoms
Income in trouble is the symptom, for which the root cause is the constraint, which triggers symptoms in other functions. Symptoms are typically resolved when the root cause has been resolved.

A living creature

A marvelously gifted being

In a systems view, the business is also a living being. It is not just a hierarchy (like our skeleton is for us) or a set of processes (like our digestive organs).

Far beyond that, it is a marvelously gifted being, autonomous in what it does, organizing itself and even capable of reproducing and maintaining itself.

It is autonomous in the sense that it can specify it own laws, what is proper for it. Its cultural values are one example of such laws, as are its operational plans, performance indicators and policies.

In system terms it is very competent in organizing itself. Every person, every function, every business unit attentively observes its environment, accumulates knowledge and is actively finding and implementing ways to do its jobs better.

Beyond that, the business system has the gift of reproducing and maintaining itself. It may create new units, like branch offices or factories. (In systems terms it is autopoietic[21])

Today is not the same as yesterday

The business system undergoes change constantly. We change the layout of documents on our desk. We arrange the furniture in our office in a new way. We change the organization. We create new products and services. We increase output in one function and quality in another one.

Elements in the business ecosystem change. Customers redefine their needs. Competitors come up with new strategies. Suppliers suddenly have a monopoly. In consequence, causal relationships of yesterday may still be valid today – or not at all.[22]

---

[21] Autopoiesis (from Greek αὐτο- (auto-), meaning "self", and ποίησις (poiesis), meaning "creation, production") refers to a system capable of reproducing and maintaining itself. The term was introduced in 1972 by Chilean biologists Humberto Maturana and Francisco Varela to define the self-maintaining chemistry of living cells. Since then the concept has been also applied to the fields of system theory and sociology.
https://en.wikipedia.org/wiki/Autopoiesis

[22] Autopoietic unities undergo a history of structural transformation, their ontogeny. Maturana, Humberto R. and Varela, Francisco J.: The tree of knowledge. Shambala. Boston & London, 1987. p.95

Not just a money making machine

It is a frequent mistake to view the business system as just a money making machine. People work in each of its functions, so of course it is also a social system. Its competence and culture (how we do things here) determine as much (some claim much more) the level of operational excellence that the business system can achieve, as the perforrmance of its physical functions.

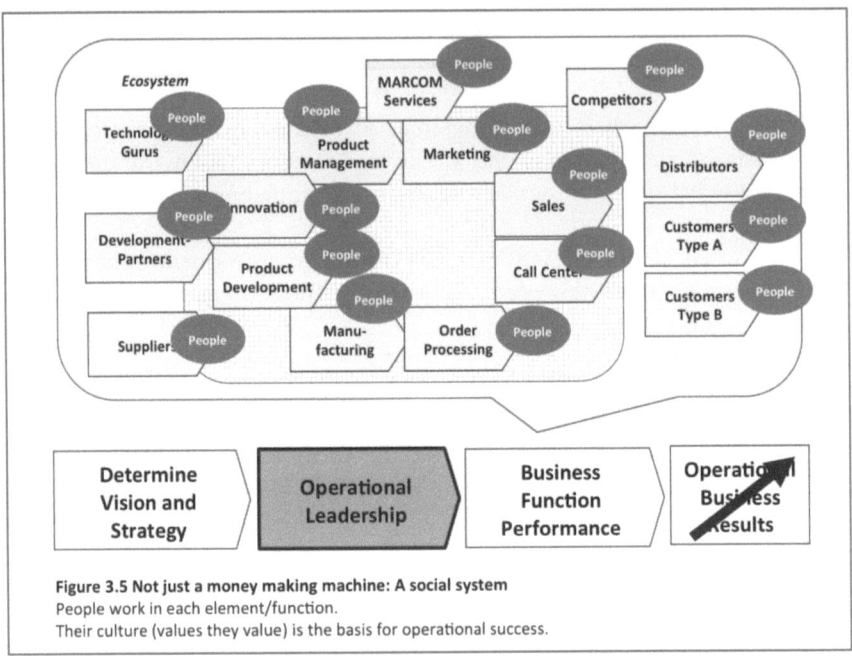

Figure 3.5 Not just a money making machine: A social system
People work in each element/function.
Their culture (values they value) is the basis for operational success.

Culture is as important as basis for operational excellence as physical performance of our functions. A low performance culture blocks a team's progress. A culture of operational excellence carries a team to success.

A culture of operational excellence is important to all elements of our operational plans. Its values should be considered as critical success factors, necessary conditions and even obstacles for progress in individual projects.

Chapter 4: Right goals

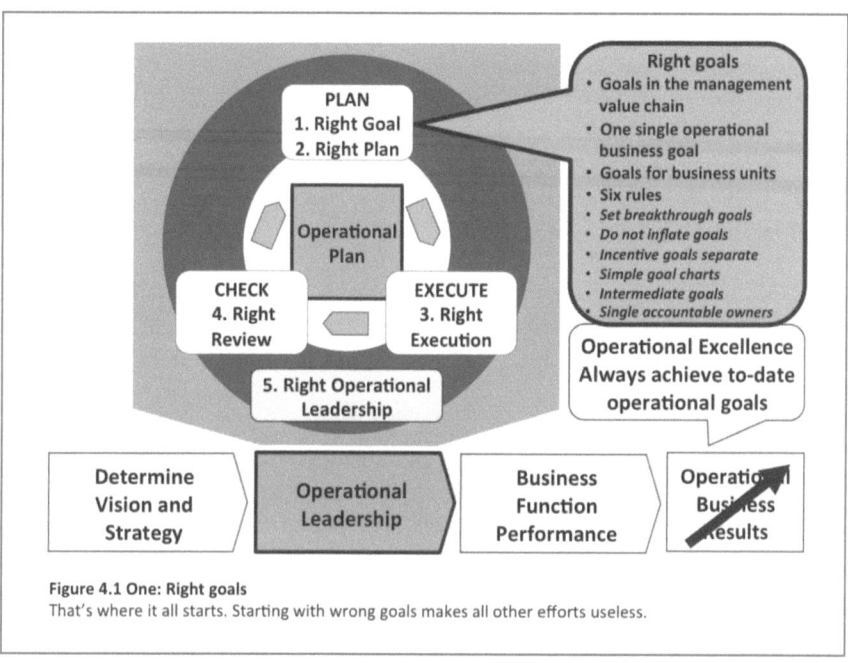

Figure 4.1 One: Right goals
That's where it all starts. Starting with wrong goals makes all other efforts useless.

Before setting goals let's agree on what is meant and the types of goals we typically see in businesses. In this chapter, we will review how operational goals differ from strategic ones and how the various goal types are connected causally.

Then, we make a bold statement: there is one and only one overarching operational goal in business: sufficient income. This one operational goal is the reason for being for all income generating business units.

The meaning of "goal"

> *If I were made emperor tomorrow, the first thing I would do is clarify the meaning of words. If this is not clear, people will be confused. If they are confused, there will be revolution. Unknown (Chinese?)*

Before discussing what should be the right operational goals it is necessary to agree on how "goal" and related terms are defined.

Goal

> *A goal is a desired result that a person or a system envisions, plans and commits to achieve: a personal or organizational end-point in some sort of assumed development. (Wikipedia).*

Goal, systems view

System thinkers call the condition of the system at a particular moment of time the system state. It is described by the values of the system's variables at that moment.

Throughout this book we will take this systems view and understand all goals as system states it is desired that the business system acquires. This is the common feature of goals, independent of what they are called in business terms: strategic goals, operational goals, key performance indicators, process performance goals, budgets or process control limits.

Goal and action

The same view dictates that we should separate goal (where we want our system to be) from action (how we get it to that goal).

Example: "Sell more" describes action, "12m$ income" describes a system state, a goal.

Objective

This term is used in so many different and sometimes contradictory ways that we shall avoid its use in this book.

Goals in the management value chain

Categorized by their position within the management value chain there are three types of goals for a business: operational business goals, functional performance goals and strategic goals.

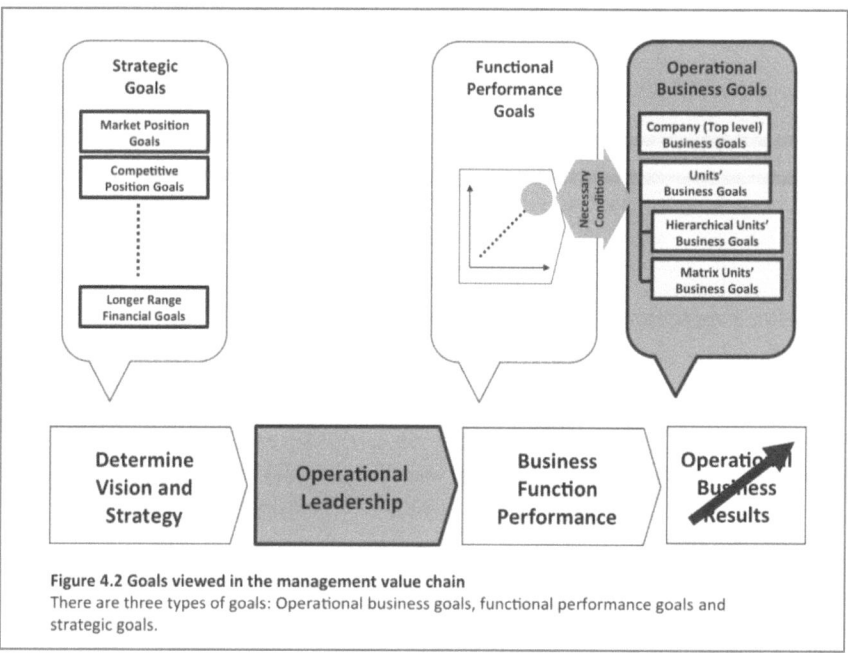

Figure 4.2 Goals viewed in the management value chain
There are three types of goals: Operational business goals, functional performance goals and strategic goals.

Operational business goals

At the end of the chain are the goals that a company is expected to achieve as a result of its operations. These are called operational business goals.

Typical examples are goals for items on the income statement and balance sheet. Businesses set operational business goals for the entire company as well as for business units like product groups or product lines.

Functional performance goals

The business system achieves its operational business goals as a result of the business functions' performance. Expressed in terms of formal logic: their performance is a necessary condition to achieve the operational business goal. ("Are indispensable for the operational business result".[23])

Necessary condition - a term of formal logic:[24]

Given two statements A and B. If A is necessary for B to be true then A is called a necessary condition for B. Example: A="Customer satisfaction", B="Sales" – customer satisfaction is a necessary condition for sales.

Also, to be true a necessary condition must be mandatory: "Sales cannot occur without customer satisfaction." (A sufficient condition in common words means "guarantees" – our example "Customer satisfaction guarantees sales").

Critical success factors

Critical success factors rank at the highest level of importance of such conditions.

Critical success factors (CSFs) are those few things that must go well to ensure success for a manager or an organization, and, therefore, they represent those managerial or enterprise areas, that must be given special and continual attention to bring about high performance.[25]

Key functions' performance

Also, if a functions' performance is a key driver for the system to achieve a critical success factor it is a necessary condition for that CSF.

Let's assume we have determined that customer satisfaction is a critical success factor. The performance level of some functions will determine whether we reach the desired level of customer satisfaction: our products need to bring value to our customers (product development); our quotations need to be accurate; our repair service needs to be fast and effective.

---

[23] Dettmer, H. William: The logical thinking process. ASQ Quality Press, Milwaukee, WI. 2007, p.6

[24] https://en.wikipedia.org/wiki/Necessity_and_sufficiency

[25] https://en.wikipedia.org/ki/Critical_success_factor

Important point: it's not all functions performing at whatever we set as performance goals for them – it's just the "vital few" (necessary conditions) that determine if we reach the critical success factors.

Obligations

The operational plan determines the system states (functional performance goals), which are necessary conditions for the system to achieve the operational goal.

For business leaders however, an operational plan is much more than a logic construct. Each of these necessary conditions is also an obligation of someone who's task it is to lead the system to that desired state as their contribution to business success.

In this book we use the following terms for the various types of obligations in operational plans:

- Critical success factors: as defined above. These are obligations of the manager responsible for the business unit,
- Necessary conditions: The conditions required to achieve a critical success factor. These are functional performance goals.
- Commitments: Conditions required for achieving necessary conditions. When commitments are delivered, we expect necessary conditions to be achieved.
- Milestones: Obligations to be delivered sequentially, both for necessary conditions and commitments, thus "building" these obligations over time.

Strategic goals

At the very beginning of the management value chain are strategic goals. These goals serve operational leadership as a longer-term framework. Strategic goals may be stated for example for market position versus competitors, or longer-range development efforts.

The longer-range financial plan, for example, comprises a set of strategic goals. It describes the development of the key financial statements of the company, income statement and P&L statement. As such, it serves as the longer-range framework for operational business goals.

Chapter 4: Right goals

One single operational business goal: sufficient income

Businesses are value-generating networks

Most entrepreneurs pursue the question, "How can I succeed?" From day one, David Packard and Bill Hewlett pursued a different question: "What can we contribute?" This was the launching pad for HP's extraordinary success. This success, in turn, enabled the company to invest even more in making a contribution, which produced even greater success, which led to increased contribution, which created even greater success.[26]

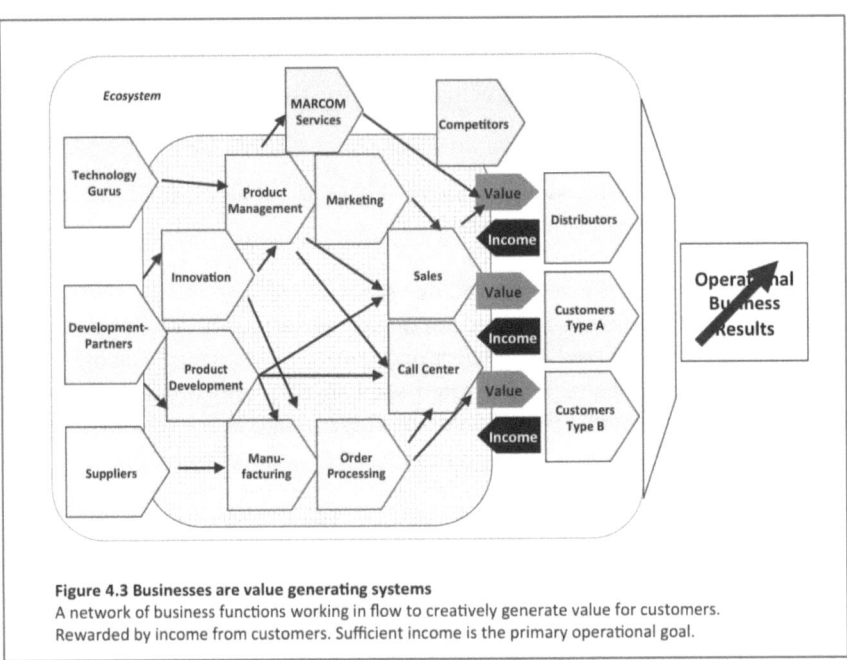

Figure 4.3 Businesses are value generating systems
A network of business functions working in flow to creatively generate value for customers. Rewarded by income from customers. Sufficient income is the primary operational goal.

As a living entity, to live and survive the business system needs energy. The energy it needs is income. The sources of that energy are its customers. They award this "food" in return for value contributed. The value contributed helps

---

[26] www.jimcollins.com/article_topics/articles/the-hp-way.html

customers achieve their operational success. Thus, the business system is a value-generating network.

Income: the money received from customers

One afternoon in Vienna, Austria, I had coffee with my friend Georg Weiner, explaining to him the wonders of management methodologies. He politely listened and then replied:

"You know, Dieter, these are great ideas – but in reality, you must follow one single rule for success in business. This eternal law for business success applies to a small shop in the Bazaar in Istanbul as much as it applies to multinational corporations. This is the law:

In the evening, you must have more cash in the box than there was in the morning.

Many managers are convinced, that this eternal law does not apply to them. They think that sophisticated management methods will out-trick this law. They are wrong. To violate this law guarantees bankruptcy".

Georg's business wisdom expresses the nature of operational business goals. Sufficient income. Just that.

Income defined[27]

Income (also called net sales) is defined as total revenue less the cost of sales returns, allowances, and discounts. (Generally accepted accounting practices (GAAP)).

Sufficient income – now and in the future[28]

The goal or ongoing purpose of a commercial organization is to make more money – now and in the future. Eliyahu Goldratt.

For a business to survive now and into the future income must be sufficient to cover
   a) The cost of generating the value offered to customers and
   b) The cost of preparing the business system for the future. In systems terms this is the cost of structural change, of self-organization and self-creation.

---

[27] http://www.accountingtools.com

[28] http://www.goldratt.co.uk/articles/Finance/measurements_that_mean_something.html

Contribution margin

The common measure for sufficient income is contribution margin: Income minus variable cost, either measured by unit sold, or for a business as a whole; in other words, what is left over after deducting the cost of generating value for the customer and for preparing the business system for the future. (Theory of constraints uses T, throughput, rather than contribution margin for the difference between income and variable cost).

Just one operational business goal? What about all the others?

Are all the other goals like customer satisfaction, market share, quality, employee competence and satisfaction, social contribution, environmental footprint, shareholder value not also operational goals? And what about the four dimensions of balanced scorecard - financial, customers, internal business processes and learning/growth?

Positioning these goals on the management value chain answers these questions: Some or all may be critical success factors or necessary conditions. High levels of customer satisfaction, product quality or employee competence might be a condition for the business system to achieve its operational business goals. Others may be goals on the strategic level, such as market share, social contribution or economic footprint, but not operational goals.

Isn't productivity an operational business goal?

Productivity is the measure of how efficiently income is used in the business system. A company may measure productivity as profit or EBIT, for example.

We could, like many managers do, define such productivity measures as operational business goals. However, a closer look will tell us, that efficient use of our resources is actually a condition for short term and longer-term achievement of income goals. Thus, productivity may be a critical success factor, or in some cases a necessary condition, but not the operational business goal for the company.

Defining increase of productivity as operational business goal may even be a significant mistake, as for example in mergers or acquisitions:

50-70% of all mergers and acquisitions are failures .. Main reason is .. Focus on cost reduction rather than growth of sales. [29]

---

[29] AT Kearney Research, quoted in Neue Zuercher Zeitung. June 23, 2008

Chapter 4: Right goals

Operational business goals for company business units

Three types of company business units

From the business system's point of view, organizational units are subsystems of the company business system. They either contribute to the operational business goal of income, or they support such income-generating units:

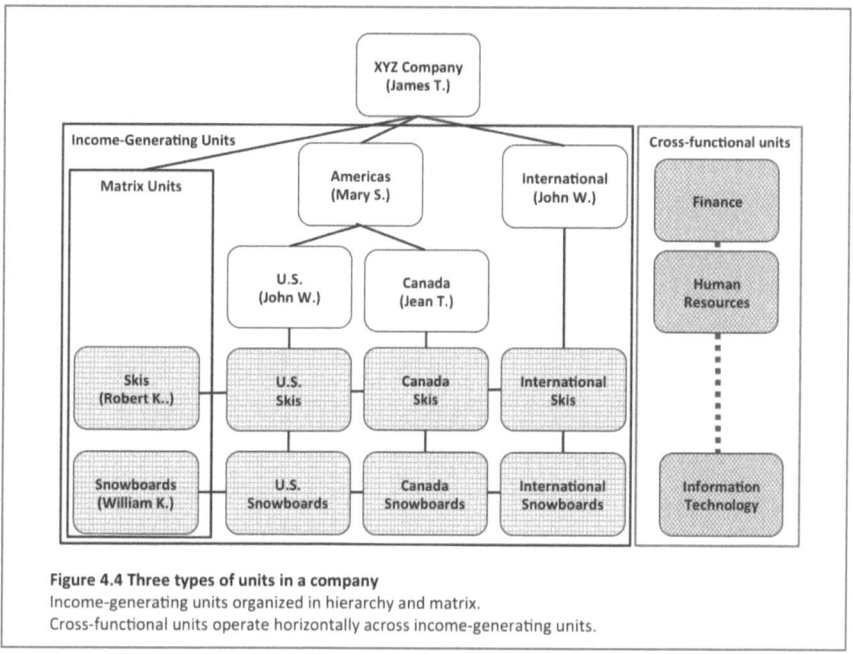

Figure 4.4 Three types of units in a company
Income-generating units organized in hierarchy and matrix.
Cross-functional units operate horizontally across income-generating units.

- Most companies organize in hierarchies of income-generating business units, such as product lines, geographies, channels, customer segments or in other ways.
- Matrix units are another type of income generating units. We set them up to focus on income of the same type across hierarchical units.
- Cross functional, horizontal or transversal units support and enable leading the income-generating units – like Finance, HR and IT. They are sometimes referred to as shared services. They do not carry goals for income generation.

Operational business goals for income-generating units

To assign and track progress operational business goals are set for each income-generating unit.

Goals for income-generating units

Each income-generating unit will have such goals assigned. These goals add up to the total company goal.

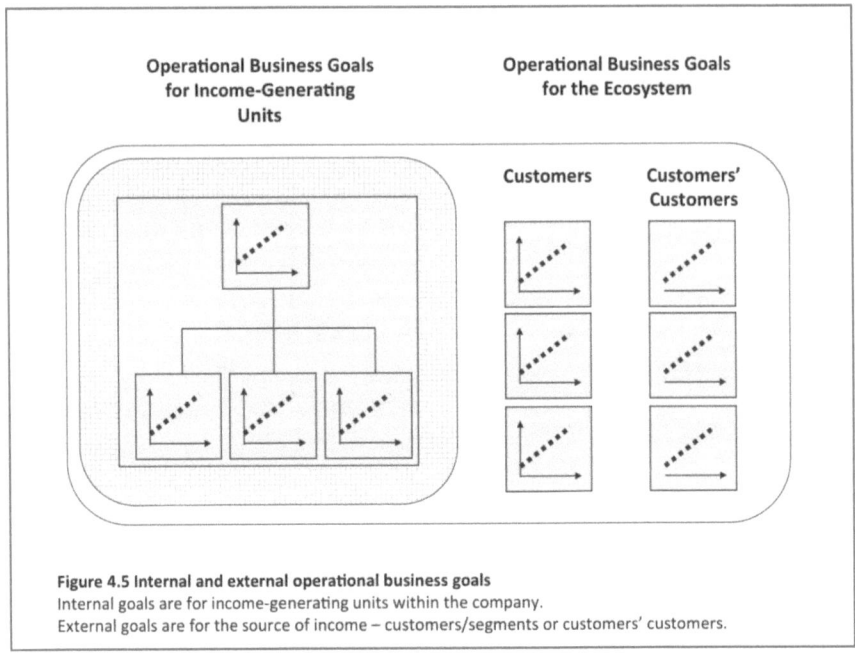

Figure 4.5 Internal and external operational business goals
Internal goals are for income-generating units within the company.
External goals are for the source of income – customers/segments or customers' customers.

Goals for the elements of the business ecosystem

The source of the business system's "food" is customers. So, there is a great deal of interest in setting and following operational goals by customers or segments.

Sometimes external goals for the customer's customers need to be considered. When printers are sold through a reseller channel, for example, goals should be set by segment of the end user customers.

Operational business goals with the right content

To serve as targets for operational excellence our operational business goals must have both the right content and be right for leading execution. Here are three rules for the right content of operational goals:

1. Set goals for breakthrough

A business operating in a market that grows by 17% per year and sets its goals for sales growth of 10% aims for the comfort zone. Such goals will not lead the business system to question its present practices.

A breakthrough goal in this case means to at least aim at growing with the market. Such goals allow operational leaders to recognize and resolve the constraints in their system in order to find new and innovative approaches for how they lead and work.

2. Do not inflate goals

In some cases managers will set higher goals for the business units reporting to them than they have for themselves. This was the approach to goal setting in the Soviet economic system.

For example, assume the goal to be 100. In the goal inflation scenario, goals to each of four units are set at 30, instead of 25. This inflates the goal for the next level by 20%. If the managers of these units apply the same practice for their respective units we quickly arrive at highly inflated operational goals.

For the people at the top this approach creates comfort – if everyone delivers their goals they are heroes, if some fail they will still reach their own overall goals. In reality, by inflating goals managers sneak out of their accountability for resolving constraints in their business system. This must not be tolerated.

3. Keep incentive goals separate from operational business goals

Some managers add incentive goals on top of operational goals. For example: "Our (operational) goal this year is to grow sales by 14%. In addition, top management has decided to set a challenge goal of 25% growth."

Which of these two goals is the true operational goal? Which of the two should the operational plans aim for? Such ambiguity confuses.

Why not say it in simple terms: "Our operational goal is to grow sales by 14% this year. If you achieve more, the company will grant a bonus."

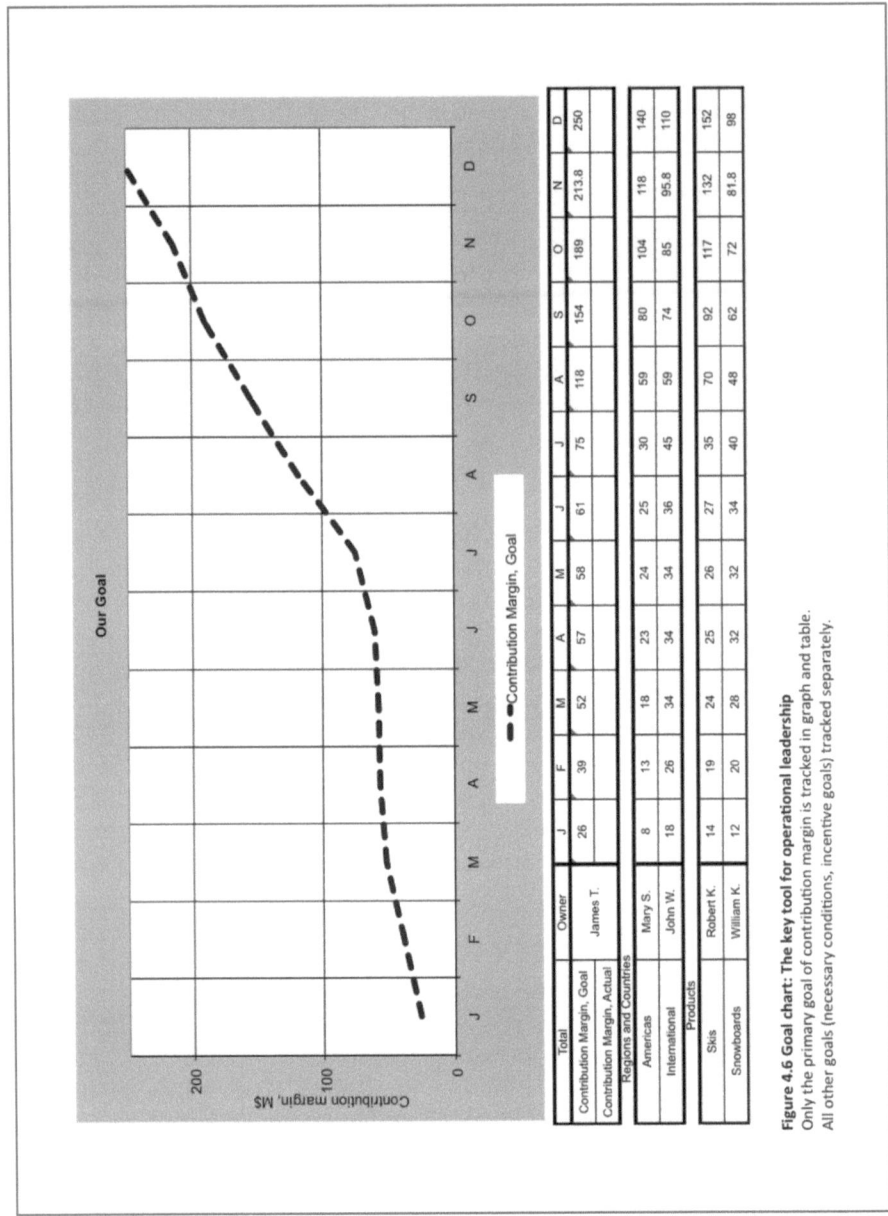

Figure 4.6 Goal chart: The key tool for operational leadership
Only the primary goal of contribution margin is tracked in graph and table.
All other goals (necessary conditions, incentive goals) tracked separately.

Operational goals right for execution

Operational goals are the guiding stars while leading the execution of your operational plans. In order to accomplish this, goals must be displayed clearly and simply and be assigned to single accountable owners.

1. Use goal charts of utmost simplicity

"It seems that perfection is reached not when there is nothing left to add, but when there is nothing left to take away". Antoine de Saint-Exupery[30]

Our people (and we ourselves) often forget our goals in the craziness daily work. An instrument is required to keep us focused on the primary task: to achieve the operational business goal. The ideal tool for this purpose is a goal chart.

To encourage absolute focus on our operational goals the goal chart must be a perfect masterpiece of simplicity and clarity. It should only show the operational business goal of income or contribution margin, nothing else. Any other indicator will confuse people. (Necessary conditions can be tracked on separate charts).

Because some people prefer to read graphs and some others prefer tables the goal chart must contain both.

2. Set intermediate goals (milestones) correctly

Set milestones

Define interim milestones (quarterly, monthly or weekly) as a basis for tracking progress. During execution you need milestones to see if you are still on track surfing your wave.

Double check hockey stick goals

Hockey stick goals are low in the first part of the goal period and then demand a jump in results in the last period. Such goals are easy to achieve in the first months of the year, but then impossible to achieve by year-end. Unless there is solid data confirming the viability of such goals, they should be avoided.

---

[30] http://en.wikipedia.org/wiki/KISS_principle

Chapter 4: Right goals

Set right goals for product rollovers

A product rollover is the process by which new products are introduced in the portfolio while phasing out old products. For such rollovers it is necessary to set valid goals both for growing income from the new product and dropping income from the product being replaced.[31]

Set right seasonality for goals

Financial planners prefer straight-line cumulative year-to-date goals. For operational leaders goals serve as primary alarm triggers. Ignoring seasonality weakens the goal's ability to act as a trigger of an alarm.

3. Assign operational goals to single accountable owners

When a team is responsible for a goal, nobody is. William Dettmer

Role	Responsibility
Responsible	Those who do the work to achieve the task. There is at least one role with a participation type of responsible, although others can be delegated to assist in the work required.
Accountable (also approver or final approving authority)	The one ultimately answerable for the correct and thorough completion of the task, and the one who delegates the work to those responsible. There must be only one accountable specified for each task.
Consulted (sometimes Counsel)	Those whose opinions are sought, typically subject matter experts, and with whom there is two-way communication.
Informed	Those who are kept up to date on progress, often only upon completion of the task or deliverable, and with whom there is just one-way communication.

Figure 4.7 One single accountable owner (RACI model)
Single ownership is a key success factor in any project.
Clear understanding of the roles in the RACI model helps ensure that roles are applied

---

[31] http://sloanreview.mit.edu/article/successful-strategies-for-product-rollovers/

Assign each goal to one single accountable owner[32]. Show the name of each in goal charts. In operational leadership team accountability for operational goals is a no-no. One goal – one owner. Just that.

Veto "TBD" accountability. If a goal cannot be assigned, make the next higher-level person in the hierarchy accountable until the position is filled.

Resolve the matrix challenge

Management brings out the best in people. Matrix management, unless managed with clear singular accountability, brings out the worst. Roger Cooper

		Hierarchical goals	
		XYZ Company (James T.) 240	
Matrix goals		Americas (Mary S.) 140	International (John W.) 110
Product Sales	Skis (Robert K.) 152	92	60
	Snowboards (William K.) 98	48	50

Figure 4.8 Goals in matrix organizations
Applying the principle of undisputed single accountability, matrix units are defined as sub-units within the hierarchy.

The need to organize in matrix comes up, for example, in sales organizations. There, you want each hierarchical unit (Regions) to aim at goals by product lines.

In this setup clear singular accountability for operational goals is of special importance. If you do not set up clearly "who calls the shots" you may end up in permanent power battles and conflicts of lines of reporting. Having two (in

---

[32] http://en.wikipedia.org/wiki/Responsibility_assignment_matrix

some cases even more) bosses telling an organizational unit or a sales professional what to do just does not work and appealing to "good citizenship" to the matrix lines does not either.

Here is an example for clear singular accountability: "For their country, country managers are primary owners of goals for both for their country and for each product line. Product line managers support country managers in achieving their product-related goals."

If you fail to establish such clear singular accountability you may have to abandon matrix organization.

Request confirmation of accountability

Demand that goal owners confirm acceptance of accountability for their goals. No goals are final without confirmed accountability.

> *You want to know why we did not achieve our goal last month, and what our forecast is? Please call my controller, this I have delegated to him. Numbers are his job - I focus on the really important things. S.R.N.*

You cannot tolerate having the accountability for goals delegated, including forecasts, of course. Not for one moment. Unit owners have committed to their goals, and that is where the accountability remains.

Chapter 5: Avoid the traps of intuition

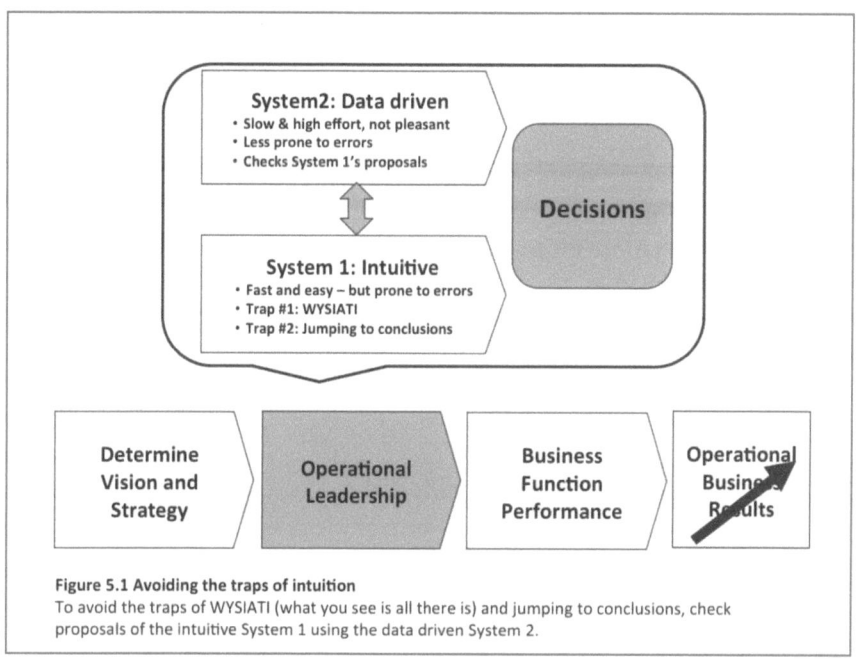

Figure 5.1 Avoiding the traps of intuition
To avoid the traps of WYSIATI (what you see is all there is) and jumping to conclusions, check proposals of the intuitive System 1 using the data driven System 2.

In God we trust. All others must provide data. Sarv Singh Soin

Goals are set, now is the time to develop the operational plan. When doing this we must recognize the limitations of intuition.

A recent book by Daniel Kahnemann[33] shows that two traps of intuition are especially dangerous for operational planning: WYSIATI (what you see is all there is), which makes us overlook essential elements and JUMPING TO CONCLUSIONS, which leads us to making wrong assumptions about the causal connections between elements of our operational plans.

This chapter discusses these two traps in detail, and how to avoid them when designing operational plans.

---

[33] Kahneman, Daniel: Thinking, fast and slow. McMillan, 2011.

System 1 and System 2[34]

In his book *Thinking, Fast and Slow*, Nobel Prize winner Daniel Kahnemann explains how we naturally use two different decision-making systems. He calls them *System 1* and *System 2*. Both are active whenever we are awake.

System 1 is the default system and uses intuition. It requires little energy to run and operates quickly. Its main source for decision-making is our model of the world, which we build from our memories. If events violate that view *System 1* asks our *System 2* for help.

System 2 constructs thoughts and decisions in a well-organized series of steps. If required, this system checks the propositions of *System* 1 for facts and data. It takes much more effort to use than *System 1*. We feel uneasy and impatient if we demand *System 2* to work too hard.

As amusing as Kahnemann's examples are, they are terrifying. They show how we are dramatically prone to errors in planning and leadership decisions if we don't resist the temptation of depending solely on intuitive planning without checking for facts with *System 2*.

Two deadly traps of intuition to avoid

The *intuitive System 1* sets up two dangerous traps for operational leaders: the traps of WYSIATI and of JUMPING TO CONCLUSIONS.

> *Information that is not retrieved (even unconsciously) from memory might as well not exist. System 1 excels at constructing the best possible story that incorporates ideas currently activated, but it does not (cannot) allow for information it does not have". The measure of success for System 1 is the coherence of the story it manages to create. The amount and quality of the data on which the story is based are largely irrelevant. ... Daniel Kahnemann.*

---

[34] For clarity we shall use italic type for referring to Kahnemann's Systems 1 and 2 in our book, and call them intuitive and data-driven respectively.

Chapter 5: Avoid the traps of intuition

Trap Number 1: WYSIATI - What you see is all there is

Priming affects perception

Studies of priming effects have yielded discoveries that threaten our self-image as conscious and autonomous authors of our judgments and our choices.[35]

The *intuitive System 1* limits our ability to fully perceive and understand a situation to just what we are primed[36] to see. It assesses a situation by recalling what we remember and what we have frequently heard. ("Anecdotal evidence"[37])

Add to this the fact that most people tell their bosses what they believe the bosses want to hear ("No problem, Boss"). This primes us to perceive reality, as they want us to see it, not as it actually might be.

In addition, consider what Paul Watzlawik calls "the group's power": in spite of being the only member of a group with the right answer to a problem, 36,8% of test persons give in and accept their group's assessment when confronted with a different group opinion.[38]

Daniel Kahnemann calls this trap WYSIATI: What you see is all there is.

Avoid the WYSIATI trap: See more than you expect

Using only the *intuitive System 1* we compile operational plans in short time, often using the BVI (brainstorm-vote-implement) approach. This way leads us right into the WYSIATI trap.

In a workshop with about 20 students from the University of Graz, Austria, we asked participants to develop an operational plan for their University. The goal: attract more students from neighboring countries. They developed their plan, convinced that it would lead the University to its goal. A group of professors reviewed their presentation. Their comments: "Sorry, but this plan will lead to our goal. You overlooked many vital pieces and most elements in your plan are not substantiated by data."

---

[35] Kahneman, Daniel: Thinking, fast and slow. McMillan, 2011.

[36] Priming is the process by which exposure to a word causes immediate and measurable changes in the ease with which related words can be evoked. Daniel Kahnemann

[37] https://en.wikipedia.org/wiki/Anecdotal_evidence

[38] Watzlawik, Paul: How real is real? Vintage, 1977.

The students used only the *intuitive System 1* in the decision making process. The professors called them out on lack of substantiating data – that is, testing *System 1* propositions against facts and data with *System 2*.

To avoid this trap when building operational plans it is important to research the entire business system (hard work for our *data-driven System 2*).

For intuitive notions we must seek fact-based proof for the validity of each single step of designing an operational plan.

Trap Number 2: Jumping to conclusions

> *Jumping to conclusions is efficient if the conclusions are likely to be correct and the costs of an occasional mistake acceptable, and if the jump saves much time and effort. Jumping to conclusions is risky when the situation is unfamiliar, the stakes are high and there is no time to collect more information. These are the circumstances in which errors are probable, which may be prevented by a deliberated intervention of System 2. Daniel Kahnemann*

The *intuitive System 1* is a master of jumping to conclusions, coming up with causal connections at lightning speed. If we let just intuition decide, the causal relationships we create are likely to be incorrect.

We are especially vulnerable to this trap at higher levels of the organization: there, we are looking back at a successful career ladder, which we climbed step by step. This confirms to our self-perception, that we are doing everything right (because we have always done it that way), and that we know everything that matters. Since nobody dares to contradict us (as bosses) we conclude that everyone agrees, and again, intuitively we are right, as always.

Ensure robust causality in operational plans

> *The confidence that individuals have in their beliefs depends mostly on the quality of the story about what they can see, even if they see little. Daniel Kahnemann*

Our operational plans are assumptions about causality. We expect achievement of critical success factors to cause our business system to reach its goals and having necessary conditions in place to cause it to achieve those critical success factors.

To avoid jumping to incorrect assumptions of causality we must again invoke our *data-driven System 2*. We need it to check every single causal connection proposed by the *intuitive System 1*, using correlation tests, Pareto analyses and other statistical tests that are available for that purpose.

Take particular care when searching for constraints

For the *intuitive System 1* it is easy to ignore data, jump to conclusions and in result to fix the wrong constraint. All such effort has no impact on fixing the performance problems of the business system.

To find the real constraint we need data that proves the causality between each individual symptom and the root cause. This requires our *data-driven System 2* to work at full throttle. And it is hard work.

Chapter 6: Right operational plans

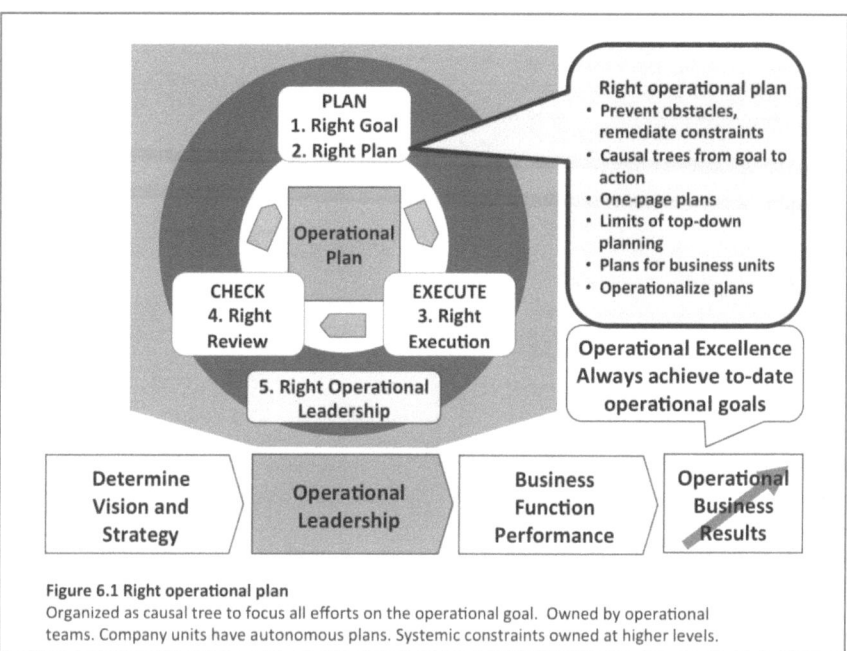

Figure 6.1 Right operational plan
Organized as causal tree to focus all efforts on the operational goal. Owned by operational teams. Company units have autonomous plans. Systemic constraints owned at higher levels.

Without operational plans our operational teams and we as managers work in a continuous fire fighting mode. Reactively we cope with one obstacle after the other, continuously multi-tasking. This is the least efficient and effective mode of leadership.

Right operational plans (our surfboards) have a few features in common: they address constraints, are organized as causal trees and are represented on one single page.

Again a bold statement: top-down planning does not result in the best plans for all units of a company. Instead, we must set operational business goals top-down, and then design operational plans bottom-up.

Two purposes for operational plans

The advantage of NOT planning is that disaster strikes as a complete surprise and is not preceded by a period of worry and depression. William (Bill) Russell

There are two purposes for operational plans:

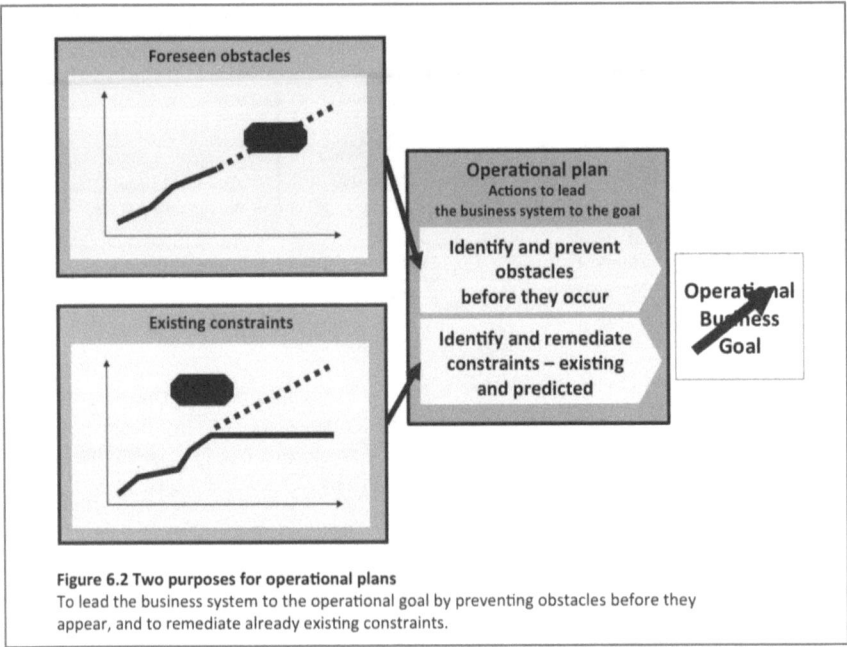

Figure 6.2 Two purposes for operational plans
To lead the business system to the operational goal by preventing obstacles before they appear, and to remediate already existing constraints.

One, to define the actions required for reaching established operational business goals. These actions are best defined by aiming our operational plans at the obstacles that hinder us from executing these actions.

Two, the system may already be constrained, suffering from a choke point. Ignoring the constraint will not make it go away. We MUST plan how to remediate it – both were it occurs now and where it is likely to move to in the future.

Causal trees from goal to action

Right operational plans are masterpieces of simplicity. They only contain elements, which will lead the business system to the performance state where it delivers its goals. All elements are linked in a causal/logic tree comprising:

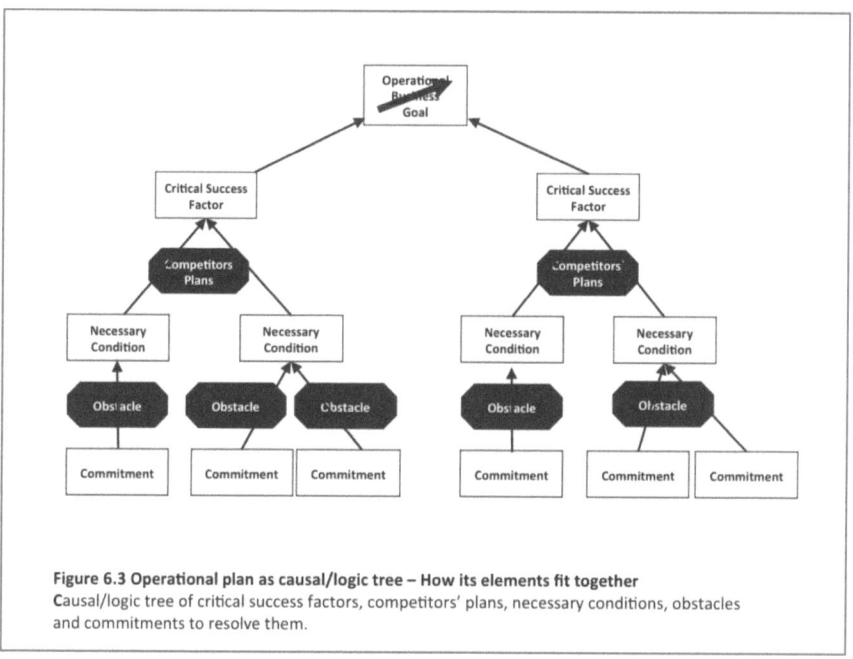

Figure 6.3 Operational plan as causal/logic tree – How its elements fit together
Causal/logic tree of critical success factors, competitors' plans, necessary conditions, obstacles and commitments to resolve them.

- Critical success factors (CSFs). Which conditions are critical to achieving the operational business goals?
- Competitors' plans. What obstacles do they impose on the business system?
- Necessary conditions (NCs). Which functions and performance levels determine the achievement of CSFs whilce neutralizing our competitors' plans? Efforts leading to NCs comprise our key operational projects.[39]
- Obstacles. Which roadblocks hinder our business system from meeting the necessary conditions?
- Commitments. Who must overcome these obstacles? How?

---

[39] Some managers call such projects mission critical. Although we agree in content we find this term overused and inflated, so recommend to use the term key operational projects instead.

Chapter 6: Right operational plans

In TOC (theory of constraints) this type of causal tree is called a prerequisite tree (PRT), as it contains all prerequisites for making the business system achieve the goal. A causal tree presents an excellent view for developing the causal structure of operational plans.

One-page operational plans

An expedition, which cannot organize itself on one page of normal letter paper, suffers from over-organization and will not succeed.[40]

Some managers find a table format easier for daily use and sharing by geographically distributed operational teams.[41]

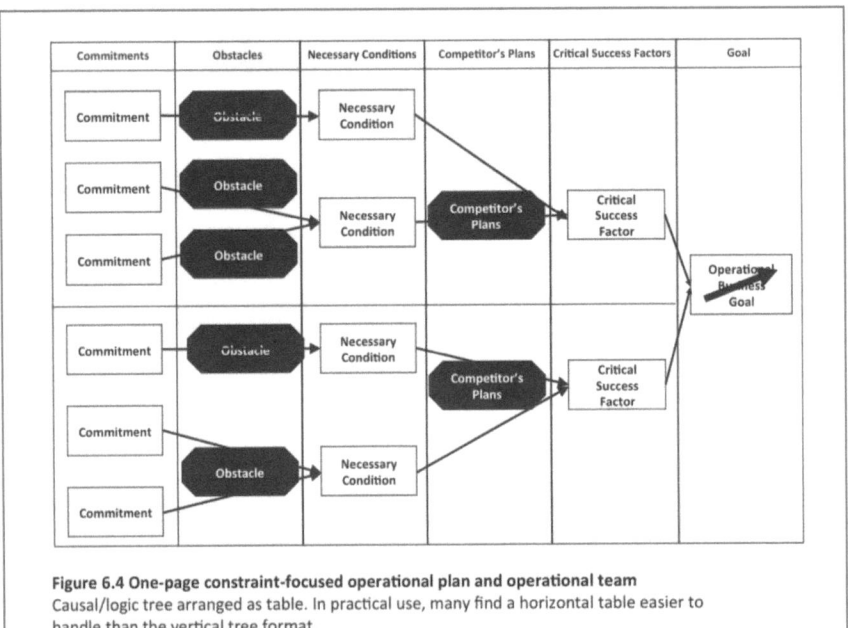

Figure 6.4 One-page constraint-focused operational plan and operational team
Causal/logic tree arranged as table. In practical use, many find a horizontal table easier to handle than the vertical tree format.

---

[40] Tilman, H.W.: Mount Everest 1938. Pilgrims Publishing, 2004. Tilman, leader of the 5th British expedition to Mt.Everest reached 8300m in 1938.

[41] The principle of one-page operational plans was first recommended to HP management by Dr.Noriaki Kano in the early 1980's and was a management practice used widely in HP.

Chapter 6: Right operational plans

Hoshin plans: One-page operational trees

The Hoshin process, which has evolved somewhat since its inception, was first used at Hewlett-Packard in 1976 at YHP, the company's subsidiary in Japan. The Japanese words Hoshin kanri can be generally interpreted as direction (setting) management for the entity. The words nichijo kanri can be interpreted as daily (fundamental) management for the entity. The blending of these two methods is key to the success of the Hoshin process.[42]

Hoshin plans are one-page logic trees. They state the operational goal and the aligned necessary conditions (in Hoshin plans called strategies) and their respective performance measures. Each business unit or department may define a Hoshin plan to focus its efforts.[43] (Michel Madec, CFO of HP France, used this example to illustrate HOSHIN planning).

Owned by: Michel Madec	Date: 1.4.94 Rev.: 01	Year: 1994	Division: Private	Location/Department: ---
Situation I am a happy, healthy person. However, I missed the plane to Amsterdam last Tuesday because I could not run fast enough. My life expectancy is lower and my chance to get sick is higher if I have overweight. My wife made comments about the fast shrinking of modern textiles.					
Goal	Nr:.	Key initiatives		Commitments
Feel physically happy, again.	1)	Eat less		<= 2000 kcal per day
Target	2)	Drink less		<= 1 glass of wine per day
74 kg by end 1994	3)	Cycle more		>= 100 km per week

Figure 6.5 Hoshin table – Example
Hoshin tables are one-page logical/causal trees containing the vital initiatives required to achieve the goal. Michel Madec, CFO HP France, used his personal HOSHIN table for training his people.

---

[42] http://www.qualitydigest.com/magazine/1997/may/article/strategic-planning-hoshin-process.html

[43] See detailed description of Hoshin planning in Soin, Sarv Singh: <u>Total quality essentials</u>. Updated edition. McGraw Hill, New York. 1992. p.73 ff.

Chapter 6: Right operational plans

Executed by the operational team

The owners of obligations in a plan constitute its operational team.

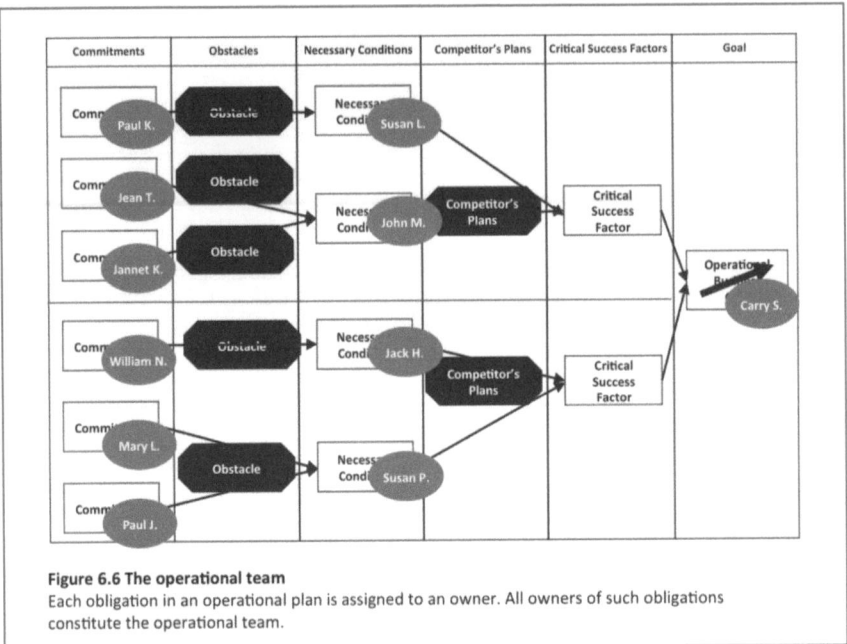

Figure 6.6 The operational team
Each obligation in an operational plan is assigned to an owner. All owners of such obligations constitute the operational team.

Even if this team may change over time the operational plan should remain in place. This is especially important when the owner of the unit/goal changes. Often new owners of units/goals are tempted to re-start operational plans from scratch, according to their own flavor.

If the operational plan was successful – why change it?

Limitations of top-down planning

The traditional approach to operational planning is for top managers to define key operational initiatives, like core themes or top priority programs. They then expect all units to implement these programs.

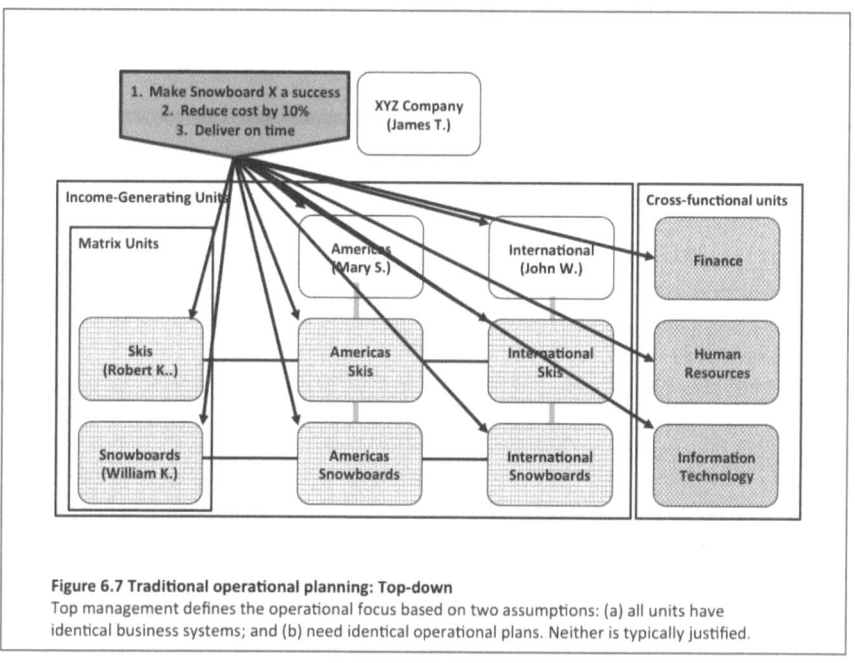

Figure 6.7 Traditional operational planning: Top-down
Top management defines the operational focus based on two assumptions: (a) all units have identical business systems; and (b) need identical operational plans. Neither is typically justified.

MbO: Top-down goal setting

Managing by Objectives (MbO) aims at setting top-down goals, derived from the company strategy. Local goals are then derived from these top goals participatively.[44]

---

[44] See Drucker, Peter: The practice of management. Harper Collins, New York. First published 1954

HOSHIN top-down linking of plans

A special feature of Hoshin planning is that these plans are linked top-down. Top management should design, from vision and strategy, a Hoshin plan for the company, and then deploy their strategies (in our terms necessary conditions) to units or departments at lower levels.

Two assumptions, neither typically justified

One year during my time at HP, the CEO defined 'on-time delivery' as the annual company focus. As European Quality Director, this was my project and I was supposed to lead it in all European countries.

Our Spanish unit just did not move, no matter how often I visited them or how often we discussed the project. Then, one day, the unit's CEO, Juan Soto, explained the reason to me:

"Dieter," he said, "I do understand that our CEO considers on-time delivery to be a key challenge. But let me tell you how I see this. Here, in Spain, we have a vital project, which is key to our future success: we are planning and building a new factory, which will add significant value, both to my country and to our company. Compared to this project, on-time delivery is of much less importance for our future in Spain. Therefore, I MUST focus all resources on the success of the new factory project. I simply cannot drive a second initiative for on-time delivery."

The top-down approach for operational planning is based on two assumptions. First, that all units operate in identical business systems. Second, that all units face the same constraints and obstacles. In a systems view, neither assumption is typically justified, as demonstrated by the HP Spain example.

What we really seem to be caught in is a misguided metaphor. This is the machine or cybernetic model of the organization, comprising a top and a bottom, a head that thinks and a body that acts, with regulated flows between them of downward command and upward results.[45]

In the example used in the previous figure, there are business units for the Americas and for International. These two markets are very different: different waves surge, requiring different business systems.

As a result, their operational plans must be different. For success they will need different critical success factors, face different competitors, require different necessary conditions and need to overcome different obstacles.

---

[45] Mintzberg, Henry: The rise and fall of strategic planning. Simon and Schuster. 1994

Thus, top-down operational planning puts unit management into a dilemma: they must choose between either implementing the locally worthless top-defined operational plans, or to ignore what top management instructs them to do and apply the Garelli principle.

The rule for survival in companies: Say YES, and do your own thing. Stephane Garelli, Professor at IMD, Lausanne, Switzerland

The dilemma is even more troublesome, when cost cutting is imposed top-down. In the worst case rather than improve things, top management decisions harm the business:

Top management in Company X issued a standard policy for all business units: "Next year, to improve profitability, 10% of the employees must be laid off – no exceptions".

In the current year, Unit A had followed a constraint focused operational plan which resulted in leading growth in contribution margin – far above what all other business units were achieving. The unit manager asked for an exception. "Did you not read the planning guidelines? It says in writing NO EXCEPTION!"

What would you do?

Neither implementing a useless plans nor ignoring top management instructions will deliver the desired results.

Autonomous operational plans for company business units

How do you cope and make sure that each unit has the right operational plan? The answer is to set and deploy goals top-down, but request unit managers to autonomously design their own unit specific operational plan.

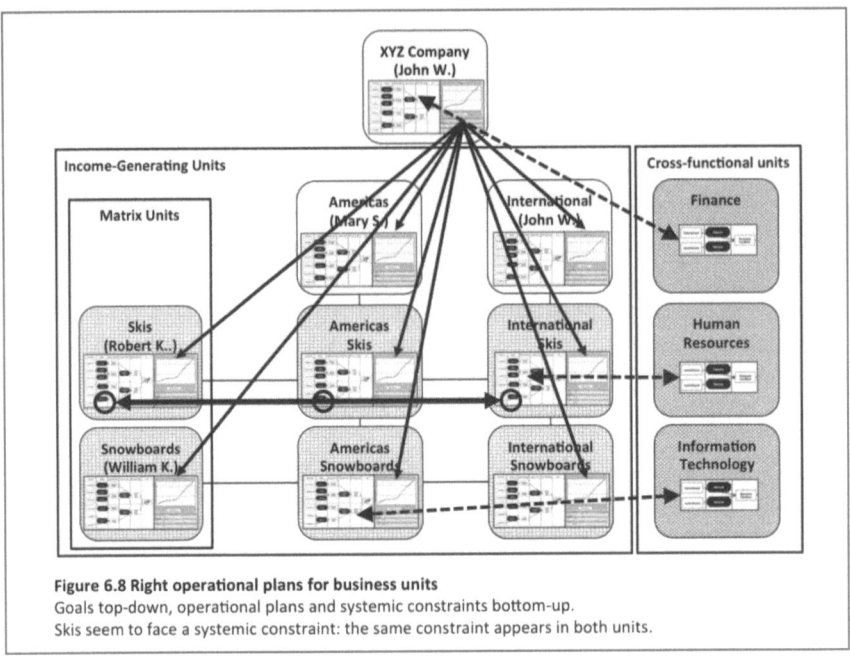

Figure 6.8 Right operational plans for business units
Goals top-down, operational plans and systemic constraints bottom-up.
Skis seem to face a systemic constraint: the same constraint appears in both units.

Set and deploy goals top-down

Keep goals and plans separate from each other. The sum of all of the business unit's operational business goals need to add up to the company's top-level goals. These operational goals must be set top-down.

Design operational plans for each business unit autonomously

Each unit team should design its own operational plan. All operational plans must adhere to the same structure – but the content may be different in each.

Admittedly this requires a high level of competence in operational planning in each unit. However, the result is a much more effective set of plans that is more likely to drive the organization toward achieving its goals.

Address systemic constraints at upper levels

Business units will face two kinds of constraints: some will be unique to the unit; others will appear in several or all units. The latter are systemic constraints, since they are barriers to reaching the goal for the whole or for a large part of the overall business system.

Systemic constraints need to be addressed at higher organizational levels – if they appear in all business units the accountability for their resolution lies with top managers. Why? Because systemic constraints are most likely caused by company policies, which only top managers have the power to change.

In company X, we had developed operational plans for five Regions. We identified local constraints for each of these units. Two of them appeared in all Regions:

a) Insufficient performance in on-time delivery resulted in massive customer dissatisfaction.

b) Insufficient speed of bringing new products to market made sales people very unhappy. They had accepted their sales goals under the condition that new products would come to market on time. Now they had to achieve their goals without those products.

We raised both constraints to top-level plans and resolved them there.

Position plans for matrix units as sub-plans

We previously discussed the potential issues with matrix organizations already in Chapter 4 (Right goals). For operational plans the same applies. It must be made indisputably clear who calls the shots.

If - as in our example – the prime hierarchy for generating income is geographic, then the goals of matrix product units are sub-goals of their related geographical business units, as are their operational plans.

This approach has a major advantage. When management teams comprised of a mix of hierarchy and matrix design operational plans for each of their product lines the so-called 'matrix conflict' disappears. Instead, they join forces to achieve their shared goals.

Define plans for cross functional business units within income-generating plans

Cross functional business units or shared services such as Finance, HR and IT enable or support the success of income-generating units.

In our example the Finance unit may support company management with a key operational project aimed at ensuring compliance throughout the company. The unit also supports the three geographical units in key projects, for which they are the most suitable owners.

To show the operational plan for a cross functional unit, aggregate their contribution across plans for income-generating units.

Operationalize the elements of operational plans

Operationalization defined

Operationalization represents a key element of operational planning.

Operationalization (or making measurable) specifies the ways in which a construct (in sociology for example intelligence or justice) shall be made observable and measurable. As basis for being able to carry out measurements operationalization is important in empirical sciences, for example when testing hypotheses.[46]

On the strategic level, like in general logic, we often do not need to operationalize ("the road is wet" may be sufficiently clear for everybody to understand).

For excellence in operational leadership however, if you cannot measure it, you cannot lead it. It is essential to operationalize the elements of the operational plans: Critical success factors, competitors' plans, obligations (necessary conditions, commitments and their milestones) and obstacles. In other words, the elements of operational plans must be stated in a quantified manner. If we do not operationalize these elements we remain in the intuitive domain and our *data driven System 2* cannot check what we propose there.

To do so, we need to define:

- Which parameter we measure,
- Which values we achieve presently and which values do we need to achieve,
- By when we need to achieve them,
- The business function where the measure is located and
- The person responsible for leading the function to the required performance.

Some examples for elements of operational plans:

Competitors' plans: Our competitors offer lower prices. Operationalized: For Product X our average price is US$12. Competitor Z offers a comparable product for US$10. (Product development; Giovanni M.)

---

[46] Translated from German original text in Wikipedia

Obligations (example: a necessary condition): Our customers are satisfied with our service. Operationalized: Our average customers satisfaction score for Service is 8.2 (31.12.2015; Customer service; Rolf M.)

Obstacle: Most of our sales professionals are not competent in key account selling. Operationalized: Of our 42 sales professionals, 12 apply our standard key account selling process successfully. (Sales; Mary S.)

DoD ("Definition of done")

The term DoD comes from the field of agile software development.[47]

In agile development, "done" should really mean, "DONE!" Features developed within an iteration (sprint in scrum), should be 100% complete by the end of the sprint.

Too often in software development, "done" doesn't really mean, "DONE!" It doesn't mean tested. It doesn't necessarily mean styled. And it certainly doesn't usually mean accepted by the product owner. It just means developed.

So, in agile development, make sure that each feature is fully developed, tested, styled, and accepted by the product owner before counting it as "DONE!" And if there's any doubt about what activities should or shouldn't be completed within the Sprint for each feature, "DONE!" should mean shippable.

---

[47] http://www.allaboutagile.com/agile-principle-7-done-means-done/

DoD in operational leadership: results – not intention or action

For all obligations – necessary conditions, commitments and their milestones – define the DoD, the end result you want to achieve. What will it look like, when you have achieved it? Only in that format you can use them as goals for your operational projects and track progress against them.

Intention	DoD (Delivered on done)
Increase opportunity win rate	**>60% win rate in A-opportunities**
Develop products faster	**<3 months for phase 1 to 3**
Aggressively market to consumers	**$15 million in sales from consumers in 2016**
Speed up repairs	**<= 5 hours time-to-repair (TTR)**

Figure 6.9 Operationalization - Intention and DoD
DoD describes the state to be achieved, what it will look like when done.
Intention describes the general direction to take. Only DoD can be tracked in execution.

Easier said than done. Our *intuitive System 1* prefers descriptions of intention or action rather than results. Engage the *data-driven System 2* to get to DoDs – as results to be achieved, with no verbs describing action. What, for example, are the DoDs of a business trip? A customer call? A product development project or a product launch?

In this case, as in others, the *intuitive System 1* does not like having the *data-driven System 2* interfere. Sometimes such interference is responded to with negative emotions. A conversation may go something like this:

> *My necessary condition is 'Make sales people more efficient'. — What would be the DoD for this NC? — I just said it. We have made them more efficient. — Then, how will we see that they are more efficient How can we measure that? — We can see it, when we have made them more efficient. Are you saying I am stupid?*

The software trap

The *intuitive System 1* loves software as an "IT silver bullet" solution for achieving a critical success factor.

To solve a problem with customer satisfaction we buy CRM (customer relationship management) software, to resolve a constraint in supply chains we buy SCM (supply chain management) software.

But which data proof do we have that this software actually is a necessary condition for achieving the critical success factor?

And: what is the DoD of this necessary condition? Certainly not "Software installed and running". For customer satisfaction, it could be "on time customer acceptance", for our supply chain, it could be "on time and complete delivery". Unfortunately, we often get so stuck in the difficulties of rolling out software solutions across the company that we forget the actual DoD – and in many cases never reach it.

It's guaranteed: whenever we define the use of software as a necessary condition we have stated the wrong DoD. The DoD is the performance state we want to achieve – not the action or software needed to get there.

Chapter 7: Critical success factors

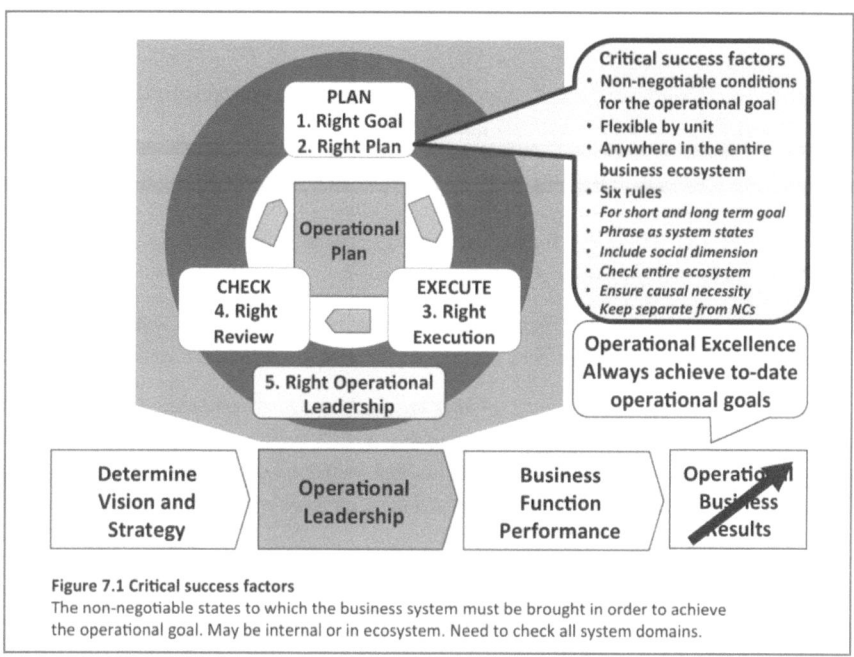

Figure 7.1 Critical success factors
The non-negotiable states to which the business system must be brought in order to achieve the operational goal. May be internal or in ecosystem. Need to check all system domains.

In the previous chapter we discussed the features of operational plans on a general level. Based on these, now we start building the operational plan – our surfboard. To begin we must define the first building blocks: critical success factors. These are the non-negotiable conditions for winning income from customers, and thus for success in surfing our big wave.

Critical success factors (CSFs) may exist anywhere in the entire business ecosystem – within or outside of our company.

Identifying the wrong CSFs will make the rest of our operational plan useless. To get them right we must search the whole business system and make sure that they are the real drivers that will lead our business system to the goal.

CSFs: non-negotiable conditions for the operational goal

Critical success factors (CSFs), as we said before, are the conditions under which customers will grant us sufficient income. They are non-negotiable – as this example from Ford shows:

Plagued with vehicle defects, Ford Motor Co. will impose higher quality standards on its Tier 1 suppliers Feb. 1. Suppliers worldwide must comply or give up the opportunity for new business with the automaker.

Ford is wrestling with a string of marred product launches and vehicle quality problems. For example, Ford had to repair more than 55,000 redesigned 2002 Ford Explorers and Mercury Mountaineers during vehicle introduction in April. The Ford Escape notched five safety recalls after launch.

Up to 20 percent of Ford's Tier 1 suppliers would not meet the new quality criteria today, said David Velliky, Ford global director of supplier technical assistance.

"Between now and Feb. 1, every supplier must go through re-certification of every one of their manufacturing facilities in accordance with Ford's new specifications," said Scott Whetter, a vice president at Siemens Automotive Corp. and the account executive responsible for global sales to Ford. "There are some criteria that could be difficult to meet over the next five months."[48]

Firm on strategic level. Flexible for operational leadership

On the strategic level critical success factors may be similar for similar types of businesses, like for profit or non-profit[49] and may remain constant for a longer period of time.

On the operational level, however, critical success factors may vary by business unit and may change over time, sometimes over night.

Different by business unit

Determined by local circumstances each business unit surfs at a different beach (different products, customers and competitors) and different (local) waves of opportunity. Accordingly, critical success factors (the conditions under which customers award us business) may well be different for each business unit,

---

[48] Automotive News October 8, 2001

[49] Dettmer, H. William: The logical thinking process. ASQ Quality Press, Milwaukee, WI. 2007, p.73

often even may vary by customer. (FORD Motor Co.® may have different criteria for its suppliers than VW ®)

Changing over time

In addition, critical success factors may also change over time. For example, they may vary as a company goes through the various stages of its business life cycle:[50]

Your business is changing. With the passage of time, your company will go through various stages of the business life cycle. A business goes through stages of development similar to the cycle of life for the human race. Parenting strategies that work for your toddler cannot be applied to your teenager. The same goes for your small business. It will be faced with a different cycle throughout its life. What you focus on today will change and require different approaches to be successful.

Anywhere within the entire business ecosystem

Factors that affect a company's ability to generate income from customers may certainly exist in its internal system, but also anywhere else in the entire business ecosystem.

Consider for example some of HP's critical success factors for going into the printer business:

---

[50] http://www.justintimemanagement.com/en/The-7-stages-of-business-life-cycle

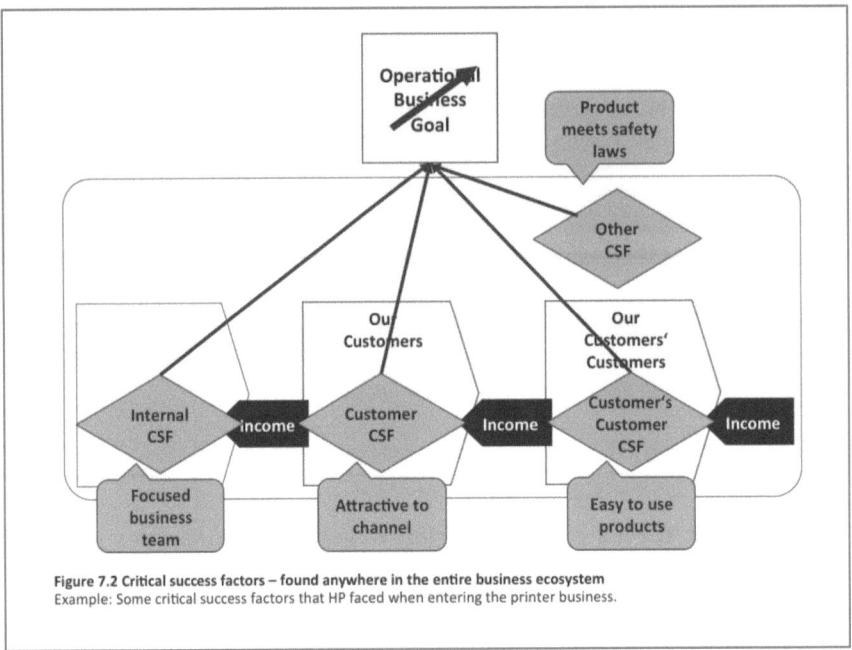

Figure 7.2 Critical success factors – found anywhere in the entire business ecosystem
Example: Some critical success factors that HP faced when entering the printer business.

- Internal: There were many new competencies required from the new business team – from product design to sales, logistics and after-sales customer care.
- Customers: When HP started that business, it soon was evident that only a channel could sell these products – but such channels then did not exist.
- Customers' customers (end users): Till then, printing was done centrally. Personal printing was new for end users. Only easy to-install-and-use products would be successful.
- Other elements in the business ecosystem: Inkjet printing brought end users in contact with chemical substances that required compliance with safety laws and regulations.

Six rules for identifying the right critical success factors (CSFs)

1. Serve short term and longer term goals

CSFs must serve both short-term and longer-term goals. Focus CSFs both on achieving this year's results and on preparing for next years' success.

2. Phrase CSFs as system states

CSFs are states or end results of the system to be achieved, not actions or intentions (Verbs) - how you want to get there. "Focus units by product line" describes action, "Highly focused product line teams" describes a state to achieve.

3. Beyond the physical, include the social dimension

As we recognized before, the business system has as much a social as a physical domain. Cultural values, as for example emotional health, need to be considered. More in Chapter 15 (Right operational leadership.)

In the example case shown later, we consider highly focused product line teams as a critical success factor for achieving our goals.

4. Check the entire business ecosystem

The WYSIATI (what you see is all there is) intuitive trap is alluring. Why not just quickly hip-shoot the CSFs and get over with it? But it is critical to use your *data-driven System 2* to not overlook a critical success factor.

Use the worksheet at the end of this chapter to search throughout the entire business ecosystem and spot CSFs related to your operational goal.

5. Ensure causal necessity to the operational business goal

To avoid the intuitive trap of jumping to conclusions for each CSF check causal necessity for the operational business goal.

Why is this CSF truly critical for reaching the goal? What happens if we do NOT reach it? Wherever possible, use data to support this critical check.

6. Keep CSFs separate from necessary conditions

CSFs and goals are directly linked in cause/effect: achieving the CSFs will result in achieving the goal.

However, watch out: Anything that is a condition for achieving a critical success factor should be viewed as a necessary condition, not as a CSF.

Worksheet and operational plan

An example operational plan

As we go through the elements of operational plans in the coming chapters we will build an example operational plan – for an invented company. This will illustrate the process of developing an operational plan, step by step.

CSFs – example

For our fictional company, here is an example of defining CSFs. We have decided on four critical success factors:

If not reached ...	Critical success factors	System domain		Operational business goal
No opportunity for premium pricing	Advantage in trends in user needs	Customers' Customers	Ecosystem	Contribution Margin 2015: $250m 2016: $280m
Ineffective market coverage	Highly effective business partnerships	Customers		
-	None	Other		
Cannot price competitively	World class low cost organization	Functions	Internal system	
Slow product cycles	Highly focused product line teams	Culture		

Figure 7.3 Critical success factors – Example
Avoid the WYSIATI trap: Consider all elements of the business system, including its social domain. Avoid jumping to conclusions: Check causal connection to operational business goal.

- The first CSF relates to the external business ecosystem. We want it to focus our efforts on understanding our customers and on meeting their needs better than and before our competitors.
- CSF Number 2 guides us to establish and lead a focused channel that outsells our competition.
- CSF Number 3 guides our efforts in establishing a highly efficient organization, with functions performing at leading cost levels throughout the business system.
- CSF Number 4 leads us to establish and maintain an organization that is exclusively focused on our product line. Every development engineer will only work on one product line, as will our manufacturing units, logistics units, sales people and managers. Not one single person and no function shall be shared with other product lines.

Chapter 7: Right operational plans – Critical success factors

Designing the operational plan

We can now start building our operational plan, by entering our critical success factors in the first column of the one-page template:

Critical success factors	Competitors' plans	Necessary conditions	Obstacles	Commitments	Operational business goal
1. Advantage in trends in user needs					Contribution margin 2015: $250m 2016: $280m
2. Highly effective business partnerships					
3. World class low cost organization					
4. Highly focused product line teams					

Figure 7.4 Designing a one-page operational plan – Step 1: Note critical success factors
Taking the CSFs selected in the worksheet, begin building the operational plan

Chapter 8: Competitors' plans

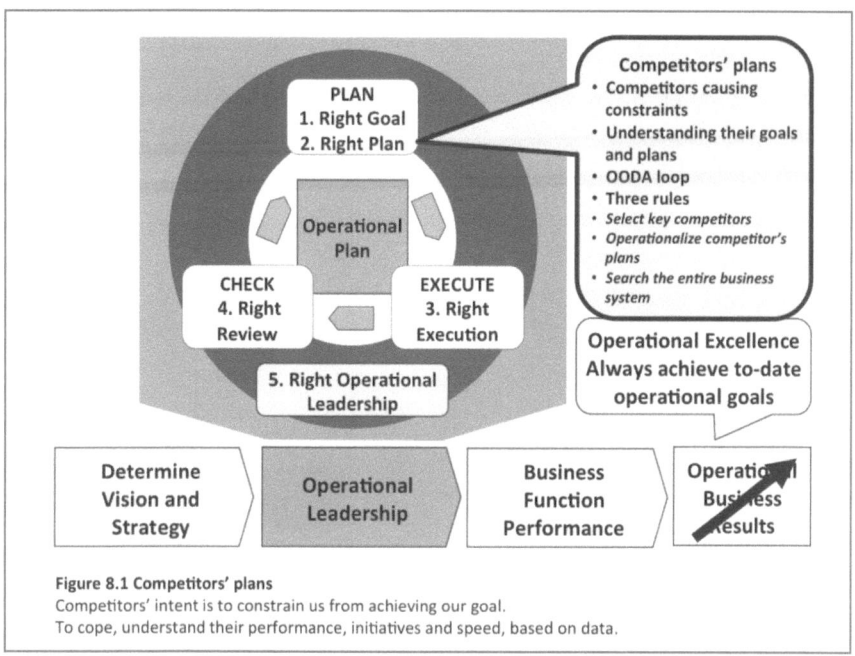

Figure 8.1 Competitors' plans
Competitors' intent is to constrain us from achieving our goal.
To cope, understand their performance, initiatives and speed, based on data.

In systems terms, the role of our competitors is to hinder us from being successful in achieving our critical success factors. Ignore them? We just cannot afford that. They are the spanner in the works; they constrain our ability to win business from our customers.

We must benchmark products, services and performance of our functions against the competition, of course. Much more important however is to foresee their operational initiatives and preemptively neutralize them.

Most important of all is to understand the speed at which they spin their own PEC (Plan-Execute-Check) loop. As we learn from John Boyd: "Every second faster than the competitor (in this loop) is a competitive advantage."

Chapter 8: Right operational plans – Competitors' plans

Our competitors – systems view

> *If you know the enemy and know yourself, you need not fear the result of a hundred battles. If you know yourself but not the enemy, for every victory gained you will also suffer a defeat. If you know neither the enemy nor yourself, you will succumb in every battle. Sun Tzu*

By selecting critical success factors you have defined your competitive battlefields. These are the domains where you MUST be successful to lead the business system to or at operational excellence.

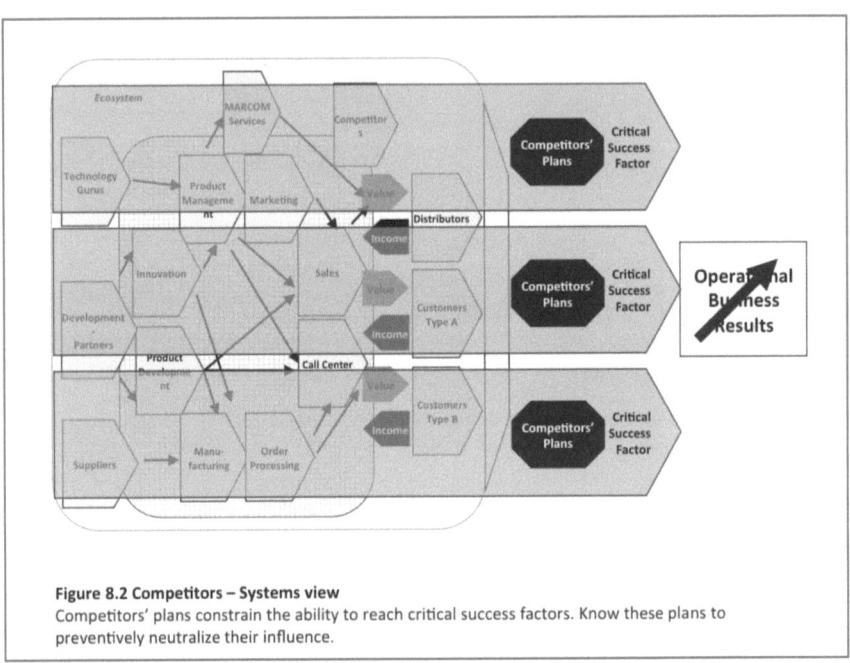

Figure 8.2 Competitors – Systems view
Competitors' plans constrain the ability to reach critical success factors. Know these plans to preventively neutralize their influence.

Enter the competitors. Their main impact is to hinder you from reaching your critical success factors. In terms of operational leadership: their efforts aim at constraining your income or contribution margin.

Chapter 8: Right operational plans – Competitors' plans

Ignoring competition – not an option

Ignoring competition is a head-in-the-sand approach and in many cases results in life-threatening danger for the business system. A famous example is the downfall of the Swiss watch industry in the 1970ies:[51]

(In the 1970ies) ... the Swiss watch industry ... hesitated in embracing quartz watches. At the time, Swiss mechanical watches dominated world markets. In addition, excellence in watchmaking was a large component of Swiss national identity. From their position of market strength, and with a national watch industry organized broadly and deeply to foster mechanical watches, many in Switzerland thought that moving into electronic watches was unnecessary.

Others outside of Switzerland, however, saw the advantage and further developed the technology, and by 1978 quartz watches overtook mechanical watches in popularity, plunging the Swiss watch industry into crisis while at the same time strengthening both the Japanese and American watch industries. This period of time was marked by a lack of innovation in Switzerland at the same time that the watch-making industries of other nations were taking full advantage of emerging technologies, specifically quartz watch technology ...

As a result of the economic turmoil that ensued, many once-profitable and famous Swiss watch houses became insolvent or disappeared. This period of time completely upset the Swiss watch industry both economically and psychologically. During the 1970s and early 1980s, technological upheavals, i.e. the appearance of the quartz technology, and an otherwise difficult economic situation resulted in a reduction in the size of the Swiss watch industry. Between 1970 and 1988, Swiss watch employment fell from 90,000 to 28,000.

---

[51] https://en.wikipedia.org/wiki/Quartz_crisis

Understanding competitors' performance

To foresee their intentions and preemptively neutralize their influence you must know the answers to two questions: Against your competitors …

1. How do your customers benchmark your products, services and functions? The answers will tell you where your customers perceive performance gaps which will lead them to give preference to you or you competitors.
2. How do you benchmark in operational leadership?
    a. How well are they achieving their operational goals?
    b. Which initiatives do you expect them to take?
    c. How agile are they? How fast do they execute? How fast do they spin their PEC (plan-execute-check) cycles?

Customer's view of your competitors

Benchmarking versus competitors' products and services

It is almost irrelevant how you yourself compare your products and services to your competitor's. What counts is how your customers rate your products and services compared to those of your competitors.

For that information you need to go and ask, by interviews or surveys, or get rated by your customer's supplier rating schemes.

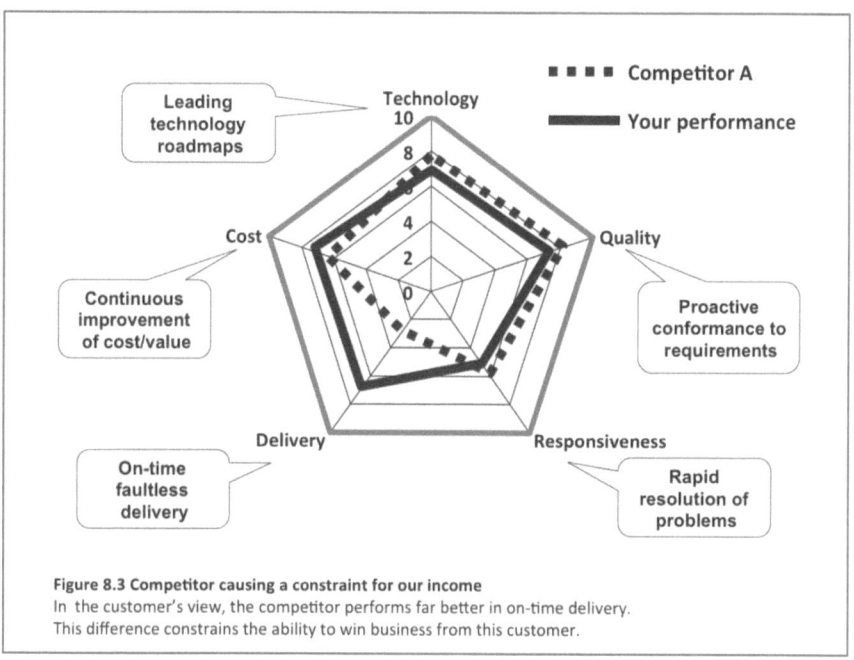

Figure 8.3 Competitor causing a constraint for our income
In the customer's view, the competitor performs far better in on-time delivery. This difference constrains the ability to win business from this customer.

In the example in the chart above a customer rates his suppliers using five criteria: Technology, quality, responsiveness, delivery and cost. We are close to our competitor A's performance except in delivery, where they surpass our performance by far. There, they constrain your ability to win business from this customer.

Competitor's operational leadership

Understanding how customers rate your competitors is key information to understand where that rating constrains customer's buying from you.

At least equally important is to understand how competent your competitors are in operational leadership: how well they achieve their operational goals, which operational initiatives they drive and how fast they are in functions, projects and their PEC cycles.

Competitor's performance in operational goals

Are they struggling to reach their goals of income or contribution margin or are they successful in reaching their goals? Depending on their situation you can expect them to drive different operational initiatives.

Competitors' operational initiatives

Where do they plan to move or move already regarding customers, markets, products, services, and functional performance? Put yourself in their shoes.[52] If you were their operational leader: Which key operational projects would your operational plan include?

Competitor's agility

You may have the best products and services. Your functions may perform even better than your customers require. Yet, if your competitors execute their functions and operational plans in a shorter time they will soon be ahead. You will fall behind, wondering what happened.

John Boyd, USAF Colonel[53] is the originator of the OODA loop, which describes how to win in competition[54]. He based his insights on his experiences as a fighter pilot in the Vietnam War and later expanded them into a fundamental of U.S. military strategy.

The OODA concept is not just another theoretical model. When used by pilots in air combat, it resulted in a 10:1 success rate.

---

[52] For a military application of thinking and planning like the enemy see https://publicintelligence.net/think-like-the-enemy/

[53] http://en.wikipedia.org/wiki/OODA_loop

[54] For a presentation by John Boyd on OODA see http://www.iohai.com/iohai-resources/organic-design-c-and-c_files/frame.htm

The OODA decision-making loop

Boyd describes a four-step process, which we go through to make decisions and act on them:

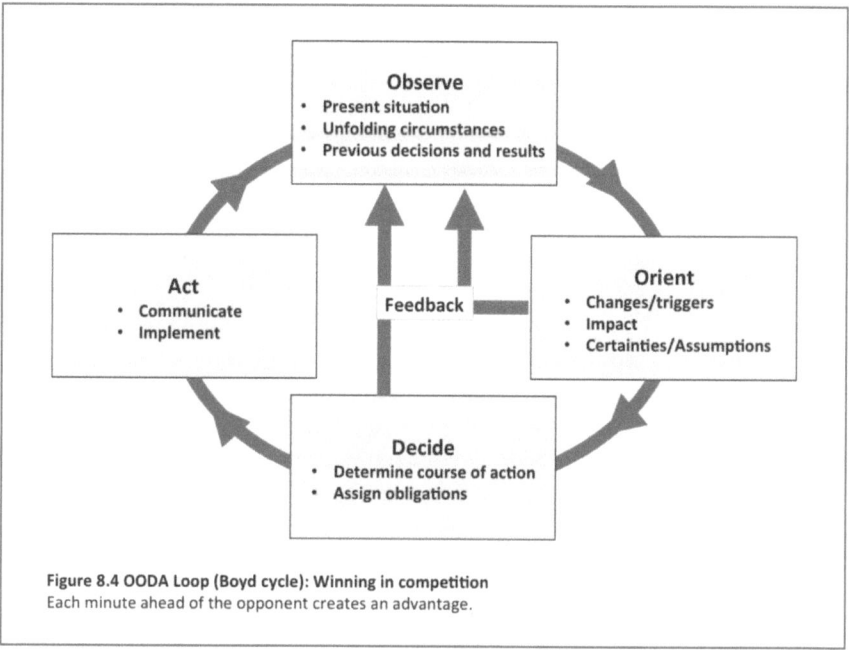

Figure 8.4 OODA Loop (Boyd cycle): Winning in competition
Each minute ahead of the opponent creates an advantage.

- **Observe** - gain information about the current situation and the unfolding circumstances. Include feedback from the results of previous orientation, decisions and actions.
- **Orient** ourselves – create images, views, or impressions of the world shaped by genetic heritage, cultural tradition, previous experiences, and unfolding circumstances.
- **Decide** – define the specific actions to be taken and assign them to accountable owners.
- **Act** – execute the action plan.

Chapter 8: Right operational plans – Competitors' plans

Boyd recognized that in competition both competitors go through the same OODA cycle. The one who goes fastest wins.

When in competition – like in military terms in air combat, a battle or a war, or in business facing competitors to win an order, become the leading supplier to a client or achieving a dominating position in a critical success factor – both we and our competitors go through the OODA cycle again and again.

> *"Time is the dominant parameter. The pilot who goes through the OODA cycle in the shortest time prevails because his opponent is caught responding to situations that have already changed."*[55]

Boyd's primary insight was that to win, doing the right things is not sufficient. You also must go through the OODA loop faster than your competitors. Thus your opponent always "trails behind" so that your moves in the OODA cycle force your opponent to go back to the observation stage while you have already acted. By turning the OODA loop faster than your opponent you dictate the tempo of the conflict. Sometimes being faster even neutralizes weaker equipment or processes. To win, you must

- **Observe faster** – perform your own observations faster, come faster to a correct understanding of the situation than your competitors and even disturb or slow down their own observation process,
- **Orient yourself faster** – come to an agreed interpretation of the information more quickly,
- **Decide faster** - define the required actions more quickly and
- **Act faster** – implement your actions faster than your competitors.

---

[55] http://en.wikipedia.org/wiki/John_Boyd_%28military_strategist%29

In business: The right things, faster than competitors

The principles of the OODA loop apply to operational leadership in several ways. To win over your competitors you must:

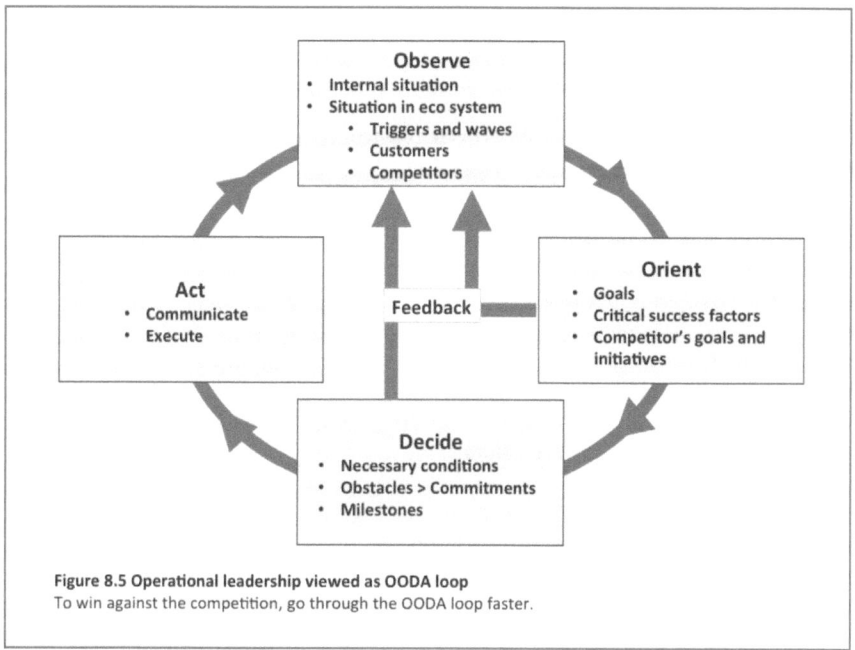

Figure 8.5 Operational leadership viewed as OODA loop
To win against the competition, go through the OODA loop faster.

- Lead in key functions' speed, for example in the product development cycle, response time to requests for quotations or delivery times. Function owners are accountable for that speed.

   To survive we must kill our products faster, than our competitors. Franz Nawratil, Executive VP HP

- Lead in speed of operational projects. Determine speed of projects by setting due dates for obligations in the operational plans, for which unit managers are accountable. Especially important is the speed at which constraints are resolved.
- Lead in speed of spinning the PEC (Plan-Execute-Check) cycle of operational leadership. Determine that speed by setting the frequency at which you review and adjust your plans. Unit managers and top managers are accountable for the speed of their PEC cycle.

Three rules for understanding competitors' plans

1. Select key competitors

You cannot observe all competitors. So, you need to select a few that you consider key. These are the ones that already constrain your income today or threaten to do so in the future. Following Michael Porter's five forces model[56], consider three types of competitors:

- Rivals: these are competitors you meet today whenever you compete for business, competing product-to-product and service-to-service (FORD Motor Co. competing with BMW).
- Substitutes: these competitors offer products and services, which threaten to replace your offer with products and services outside of your present portfolio, as for example CAR2GO[57] offering an alternative to using your own car.
- New entrants: these competitors are new in the market, as for example HP entering the multi-user computer market (in 1972), where IBM already was an established player.

2. Operationalize competitors' plans

Data, not anecdotes

When trying to understand competitors, in seconds, the *intuitive System 1* offers stories it remembers. "These guys always give more discount." - "Their products are superior technology, ours are behind." - "They produce to stock, so they can deliver faster." - "They have twice as many sales people as we have".

This may be so, but for building an effective operational plan such anecdotal information is insufficient. You need data (*data-driven System 2* checking):

- Always more discount? How much, case by case where we competed in the last 12 months? For which products?
- Superior technology? What difference in performance, expressed in data? What is their product road map?
- Produce to stock? Which model? How much do they have in stock?
- Twice as many sales people? How many sales people? In which market(s)?

---

[56] https://en.wikipedia.org/wiki/Porter_five_forces_analysis
[57] https://www.car2go.com/en/austin/how-does-car2go-work/

Competitor's speed

To aim the operational plan at preempting or neutralizing competitors' moves it is important to understand the speed at which they perform their functions and spin their PEC cycles. You need to operationalize descriptions of competitors' speed. Three examples:

They issue quotes faster. Better: Their sales people issue quotes when meeting the customer, we take 3 days.

They are slow in product development. Better: In product development, they perform an annual cycle. Our cycle is 6 months.

They implement software fast. Better: To implement the XYZ software they took 12 months, we took 24 months.

3. Search the entire business ecosystem

To ensure that you do not fall into the intuitive trap of WYSIATI engage *data-driven System 2* and check each element of their business system.

Worksheet and operational plan

The worksheet included here will help you check their entire business system while relating competitors' functions to your critical success factors. For each, note where you know or expect them to lead performance, at which speed. Our example gives values for two competitors, (A) and (B). Note that for our CSF "Advantage in trend in user needs" we have selected two items related to speed of key functions.

After completing the check across the competitor's business system you can further complete the one-page operational plan.

Chapter 8: Right operational plans – Competitors' plans

	Ecosystem		Competitors' performance and plans in their related business functions					Critical success factors
					Internal system			
Suppliers	Enablers	Customers	Op. Leadership	Service	Supply Chain	Sales&Mktg	Products	
				(B) Perf.Goal: Top service rating >TTF < 3 days (ongoing) > 65% parts on stock (12-15)			(A) Perf.Goal: Stable 12 mths product development cycle ongoing	1. Advantage in trends in user needs
						(B) Perf. Goal: $8m sales/head >50/50 incentive scheme >Sales work from home Both ongoing		2. Highly effective sales function
					(B): Perf.Goal: Final configuration ex works >Customer config via Web (06-15)			3. World class low cost organization
			(A),(B) Perf.Goal: Profit by country Ongoing. No plans for separate units by product lines.					4. Highly focused product line teams
(A) Perf.Goal: Cost of material < 15% > New supplier contracts (12-15)								

Figure 8.6 Understanding competitors' operational performance and speed - Worksheet
Whole systems check – which of their functions relate to critical success factors? Which performance goals do they aim for? Which change initiatives are they planning? How fast are they?

Commitments	Obstacles	Necessary conditions	Competitors' plans	Critical success factors	Operational business goal
			(A) Perf.Goal: Stable product development cycle > 12 mths, ongoing	1. Advantage in trends in user needs	
			(B) Perf.Goal: Top service rating > TTF < 3 days (ongoing) > 65% parts on stock (12-15)		
			(B) Perf. Goal: >$8m sales/head >50/50 incentive scheme >Sales work from home Both ongoing	2. Highly effective sales function	Contribution margin 2015: $250m 2016: $280m
			(A) Perf.Goal: Cost of material < 15% > New supplier contracts (12-15)	3. World class low cost organization	
			(B): Perf.Goal: Final configuration ex works > Customer config via Web (06-15)		
			(A),(B) Perf.Goal: Profit by country, ongoing. No plans for separate units by product lines.	4. Highly focused product line teams	

Figure 8.7 Designing our operational plan - Step 2: Note key competitors' plans
Performance and speed in competitors' functions, as related to our critical success factors.

Chapter 9: Necessary conditions

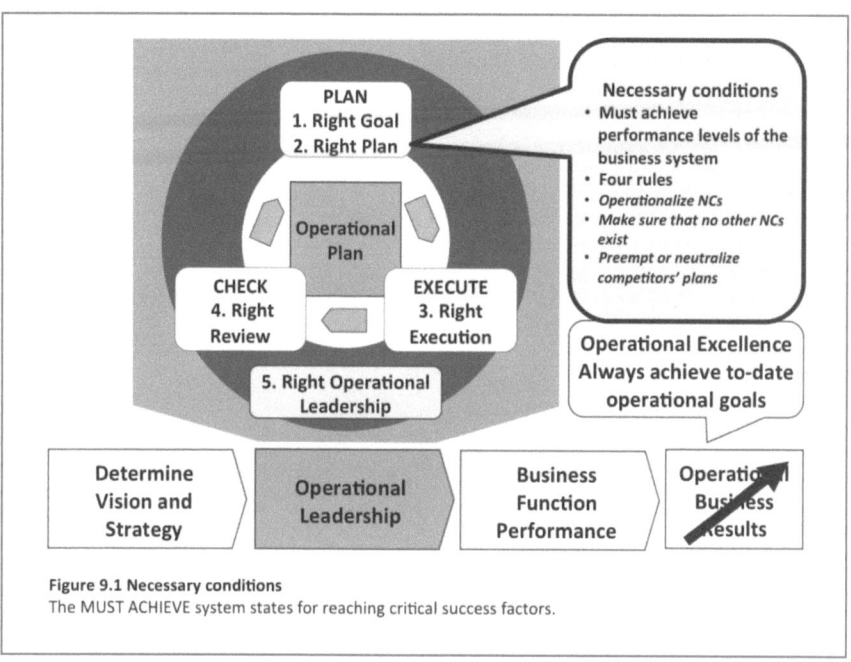

Figure 9.1 Necessary conditions
The MUST ACHIEVE system states for reaching critical success factors.

Your operational plan (your surfboard) comprises the key operational projects required to bring the business system to a state where it achieves its goals. The goals of these projects are states of our business system and the conditions that are necessary to bring it to our critical success factors.

It is essential to establish the right necessary conditions (NCs) – a wrong NC will send people after an operational red herring – wasting company time and effort and leading nowhere in the quest to achieve CSFs.

Following four rules outlined in this chapter helps in defining the right necessary conditions.

MUST ACHIEVE performance levels of the business system

In operational planning necessary conditions are performance levels you must lead the business to achieve in order to reach its critical success factors while neutralizing or preempting constraints imposed by competitors.

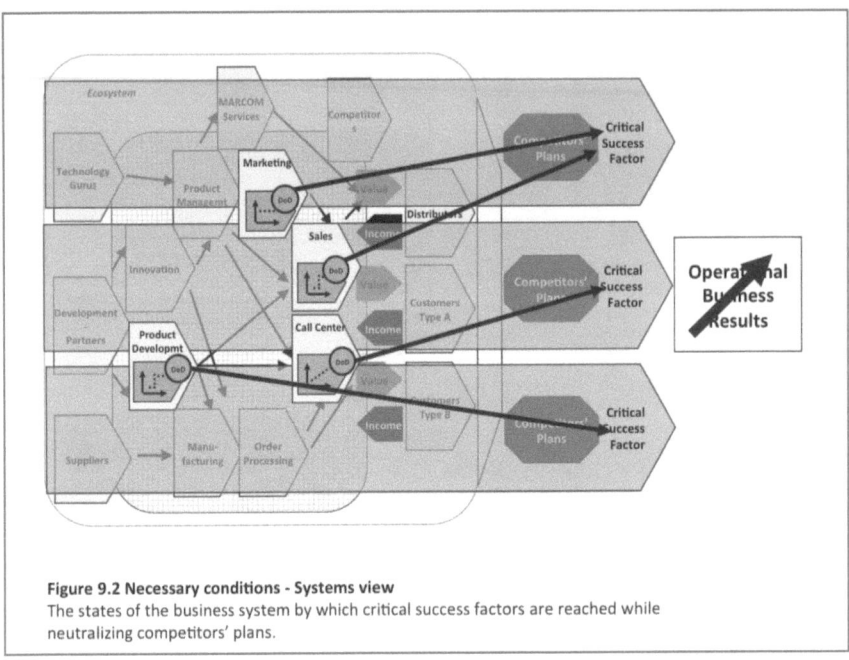

Figure 9.2 Necessary conditions - Systems view
The states of the business system by which critical success factors are reached while neutralizing competitors' plans.

As we discussed in Chapter 4 (Right goals/Functional performance goals) these levels are system states.

Another term for these states could be key performance indicators (KPIs), as they are the keys to success. However, this term has been overused and inflated, and does not express the logic rigor required. Therefore it is preferable to use the term proposed by TOC (theory of constraints), necessary condition (abbreviated NC), which is also the term used in formal logic.

Four rules for setting right NCs

To be correctly defined necessary conditions in operational plans must meet four criteria:

1. Operationalize necessary conditions

Define clear DoDs

As system states NCs need to be phrased as DoDs, not as initiatives (verbs).

Define responsible function

A necessary condition is always assigned to one of the business system's functions. This function must be explicitly named. This also defines the accountable owner of the NC.

Assign NC to single accountable owner

Assume you want to improve availability of spare parts for one product in a country. It is tempting to assign the job to a committee of the three persons responsible for service, product and country. To avoid the term committee we could call it a team – it is still the same. Unfortunately, committees are incapable of leading such projects to success.

Only single accountable project leaders can do this job. (See definition of accountable owner in Chapter 4 (Right goal/RACI model).

Assign NC at right level

If, for example, the necessary condition requires creating a new sales channel you can't expect a sales professional to lead that key operational project to success.

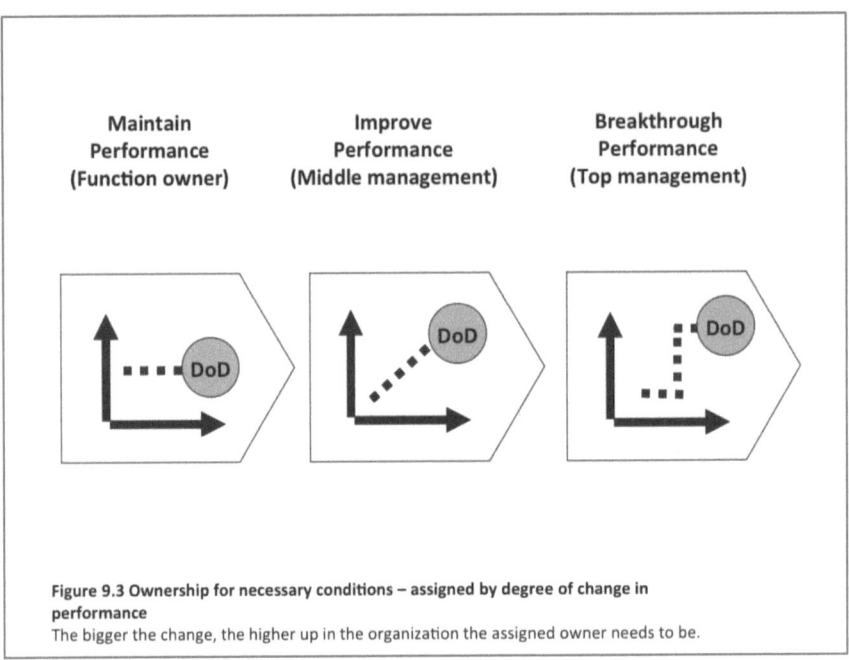

Figure 9.3 Ownership for necessary conditions – assigned by degree of change in performance
The bigger the change, the higher up in the organization the assigned owner needs to be.

NCs need to be assigned by the degree of change they demand from the business system. The bigger the change required, the more and complex obstacles will be faced and the higher up in the organization the ownership must be assigned.

Define milestones

To lead through the required change, track progress against NCs, with milestones. Some NCs will be tracked monthly, highly critical ones require weekly or even daily milestones.

It is a good practice to use tracking charts for NCs. These show goals and performance in their DoDs with both a line chart and in a table.

2. Prove causal connection to CSF

The jumping to conclusions trap is wide open. "Obviously this is a necessary condition for our CSF," is a common refrain.

Incorrect causal connection means that the NC is wrong and all effort to achieve it will be wasted. Double-check the causal connection between a proposed NC and the related critical success factor. Is it truly a necessity? Can the CSF truly not be attained unless this NC is achieved?

3. Make sure that you identified all NCs

Once one necessary condition has been identified the *intuitive System 1* immediately interferes: "That's enough. Let's continue." And this leads right into the WYSIATI (what you see is all there is) trap.

To avoid that and make sure that you have not overlooked an NC, check all functions of the business system. The worksheet provided later in this chapter can be used to deploy your CSFs to all functions of the business system. This enables a complete check for necessary conditions.

4. Preempt or neutralize competitors' plans

> *If your enemy is secure at all points, be prepared for him. If he is in superior strength, evade him. If your opponent is temperamental, seek to irritate him. Pretend to be weak, that he may grow arrogant. If he is taking his ease, give him no rest. If his forces are united, separate them. If sovereign and subject are in accord, put division between them. Attack him where he is unprepared, appear where you are not expected. Sun Tzu, The Art of War*[58]

To neutralize competitors' plans set necessary conditions for superior performance and speed both in key functions and operational projects.

---

[58] http://www.goodreads.com/work/quotes/3200649

Aim for superior performance

Aim for superior performance in functions by either setting a higher goal ("They take 12 months, so we will take 6 months to develop a new product.") or by setting one that makes our competitor's performance irrelevant. ("They have a geographic sales force, we organize sales by accounts.")

Plan to move faster

As we saw from the discussion about the OODA loop, operational speed is key for preempting competitors' plans. The due dates set for necessary conditions determine that speed.

Worksheet and operational plan

Our NC worksheet can be used to check for NCs throughout the entire business system – by critical success factor and competitors' plans.

The NCs identified are then entered into the one-page plan, aligned to their critical success factors and the related plans of our competitors.

Chapter 9: Right operational plans – Necessary conditions

Cultural domain	External system			Necessary conditions						Critical success factors	Operational Business Goal
	Suppliers	Enablers	Customers	Op. Leadership Edward E.	Service Thomas T.	Internal system Supply Chain William W.	Sales & Mktg Frank F./Mary M.	Product Dev't James T.	Competitors		
					< 8 hours time to fix IP (03-16)			< 6 months new product cycle BT (01-16)	(A) Perf Goal: Stable product development cycle > 12 mths, ongoing	1. Advantage in trends in user needs	
							Marketing: >15% RFQs by web marketing BT (12-15)		(B) Perf Goal: Top service rating > TTF < 3 days (ongoing) > 65% parts on stock (12-15)		
							Sales: $60m key account sales IP (PY-16)		(B) Perf Goal: $8m sales/head >50/50 incentive scheme >Sales work from home Both ongoing	2. Highly effective sales function	
				< $25m COGS IP (12-15)		Inventory driven cost < 14% of revenue IP (03-16)			(A) Perf Goal: Cost of material < 15% > New supplier contracts (12-15)	3. World class low cost organization	
									(B) Perf Goal: Final configuration on works > Customer config via Web (06-15)		
				Separate organizations for value chains of PL A and B BT (07-15)					(A)(B) Perf Goal: Profit by country Ongoing. No plans for separate units by product lines.	4. Highly focused product line teams	Contribution margin: 2015: $250m 2016: $280m

Figure 9.4 Defining necessary conditions - Worksheet (Example)
The key performance indicators defined for competitive differentiation within critical success factors. Entire ecosystem (both internal and external) and cultural domain are checked.

Chapter 9: Right operational plans – Necessary conditions

Commitments	Obstacles	Necessary conditions	Competitors' plans	Critical success factors	Operational business goal
		1.1 Product development: < 6 months new product cycle James T. BT (01-2016)	(A) Perf.Goal: Stable product development cycle > 12 mths, ongoing	1. Advantage in trends in user needs	Contribution margin 2015: $250m 2016: $280m
		1.2 Service: > 8 hours time to fix Thomas T. IP (03-16)	(B) Perf.Goal: Top service rating > TTF < 3 days (ongoing) > 65% parts on stock (12-15)		
		2.1 Marketing: +15% RFQs by web marketing Mary M. BT (12-15)	(B) Perf. Goal: $8m sales/head >50/50 incentive scheme >Sales work from home Both ongoing	2. Highly effective sales function	
		2.2 Sales: $60m key account sales Frank F. IP (FY-16)			
		3.1 Manufacturing: < $25m COGS Edward E. IP (12-15)	(A) Perf.Goal: Cost of material < 15% > New supplier contracts (12-15)	3. World class low cost organization	
		3.2 Supply chain: Inventory driven cost < 14% of revenue William W. IP (03-16)	(B): Perf.Goal: Final configuration ex works > Customer config via Web (06-15)		
		4.1 Company management: Separate organizations for value chains of Pl. A and B Edward E. BT (07-15)	(A),(B) Perf.Goal: Profit by country, ongoing. No plans for separate units by product lines.	4. Highly focused product line teams	

Figure 9.5 Designing the operational plan – Step 3: Note necessary conditions
Expanding the plan's causal tree by adding the necessary conditions – through competitors' plans – to the critical success factors.

Chapter 10: Obstacles

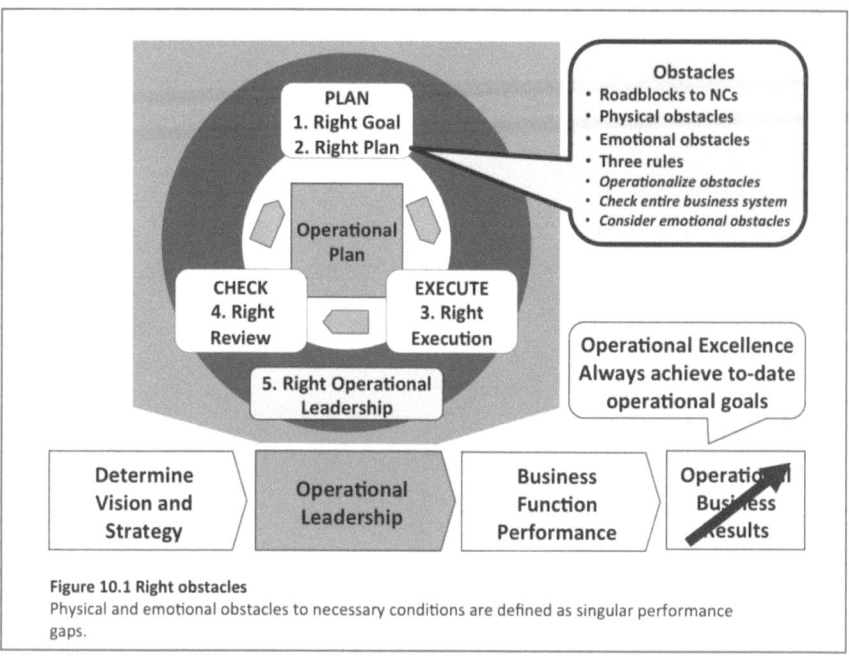

Figure 10.1 Right obstacles
Physical and emotional obstacles to necessary conditions are defined as singular performance gaps.

Of course, for any change in a business system there are obstacles to overcome. The ones to really worry about are those that prevent reaching necessary conditions.

Physical obstacles may appear in any function of the business ecosystem. The ones often ignored are the emotional obstacles, which are the most obstructive if the change you want to achieve is big.

Three rules must be followed in defining the right obstacles.

Obstacle, defined

Obstacles are states of the business system that hinder achievement of necessary conditions' DoD (Definition of Done).

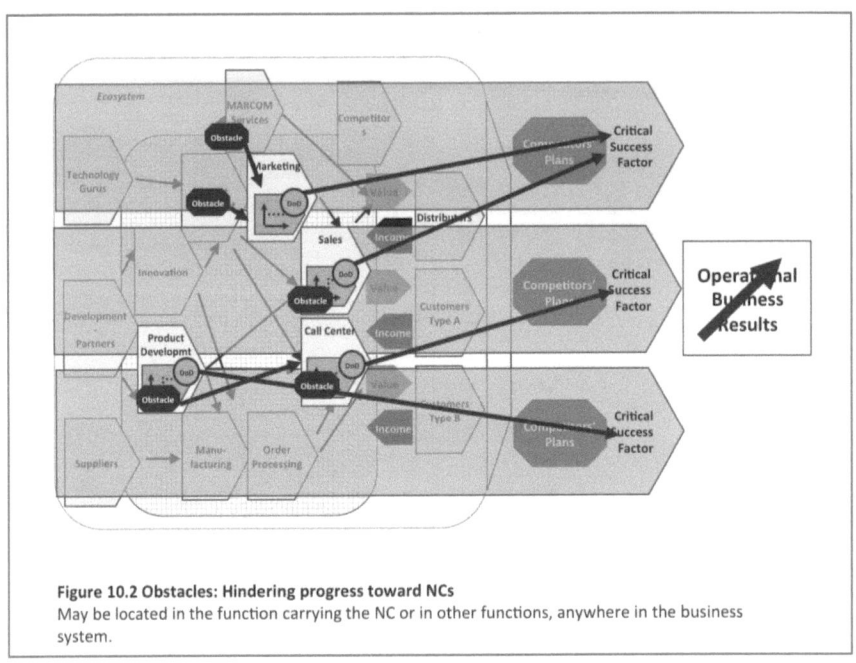

Figure 10.2 Obstacles: Hindering progress toward NCs
May be located in the function carrying the NC or in other functions, anywhere in the business system.

An obstacle (also called a barrier, impediment or stumbling block) is an object, thing, action or situation that causes an obstruction. There are, therefore, different types of obstacles, which can be physical, economic, bio psychosocial, cultural, political, technological or even military.[59]

Failure to identify and resolve "show stopping obstacles" can bring execution of an operational plan to a complete halt.[60]

---

[59] https://en.wikipedia.org/wiki/Obstacle

[60] Dettmer, H. William: The logical thinking process. ASQ Quality Press, Milwaukee, WI. 2007, p.270

Physical obstacles

Physical obstacles are physical limitations of the business system's functions, like for example lack of capacity or competence to perform at the level required for achieving necessary conditions.

Policies as obstacles

Ninety percent of what we call management consists of making it difficult for people to get things done. Peter Drucker (quoted by Hans-Peter Liebmann)

Physical obstacles are actually often caused by management policy. Example: According to its financial policy, a company measures efficiency in cost per dollar by period. This limits its ability to manage big projects, where expenses and return do not appear in the same period. No matter how hard the people in sales and project consulting work, they cannot improve unless the accounting policy is adjusted. This is not a matter of having made wrong decisions. It just cannot be avoided that a policy, which served its purpose yesterday, today turns into an obstacle under changed conditions.

The solutions of yesterday's problems often are the problems of tomorrow. Manuel Diaz[61]

Emotional obstacles[62]

I admit: I was close to giving up. HP Europe's management had promoted me to Director of Quality. I had worked hard to design a project plan. I had presented it at every level of the organization. We even had commissioned a cost of non-conformance study, which proved that we wasted a large part of our cost due to quality problems.

Everyone had agreed, but nobody moved. Not even by an inch. Then, I met Branka Zei-Pollermann, expert in emotional decision-making.

"Dieter," she said, "With your engineer's mind, you view projects as rational challenges. You ignore that there are emotional obstacles. If such obstacles exist they block your projects just like rational reasons."

---

[61] Manuel F. Diaz, head of Worldwide Sales for Hewlett-Packard's (HP) Computer Systems Organization (now retired)

[62] I am very grateful to Dr.Branka Zei-Pollermann, head of VOX Institute Geneva (Switzerland) for coaching me on emotional obstacles and decision making.

Physical obstacles come up, when a function fails to perform as required for reaching a necessary condition. Emotional obstacles exist, when individual owners or teams emotionally decide to not engage in the required action.[63]

How we decide emotionally

To better understand how emotional obstacles arise in people let's have a look at the process by which they decide in the emotional domain.

To arrive at an emotional "Yes, will do" or "No", people evaluate the emotional impact of the request to deliver a necessary condition (a 'trigger', in psychological terms.)

Branka Zei-Pollermann researched this evaluation process for many years, testing her findings with several thousand persons worldwide. She found, that people evaluate triggers emotionally by 16 criteria, of which four are most determining.[64]

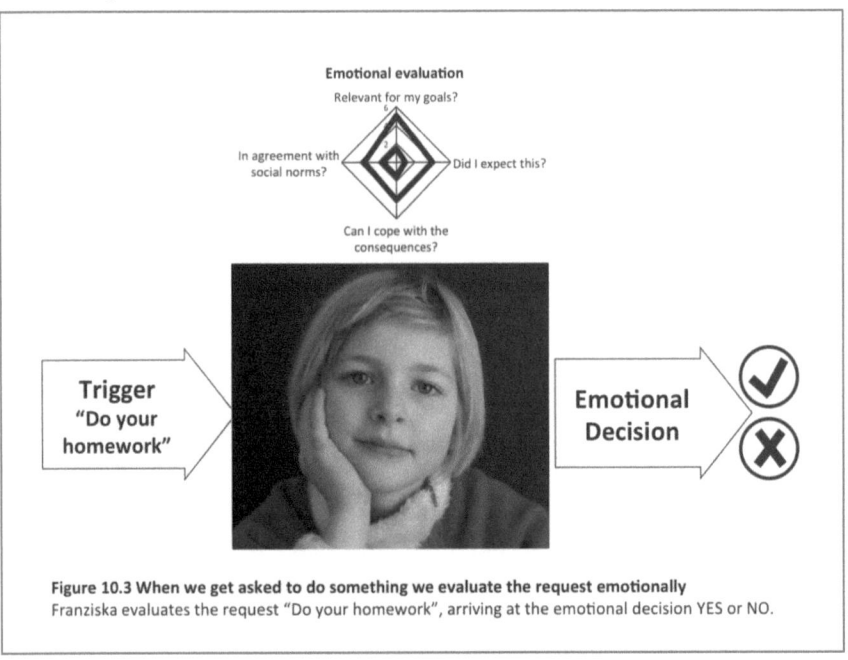

Figure 10.3 When we get asked to do something we evaluate the request emotionally
Franziska evaluates the request "Do your homework", arriving at the emotional decision YES or NO.

---

[63] For a wider view of emotional decision making see presentation by Branka Zei-Pollermann at University of Louvain, 2006

[64] We will relate to this as Zei-Pollermann model in further chapters

Franziska, the girl in the illustration, will start her evaluation by asking, "Is this relevant for my intentions or goals?" If she perceives the request to do her homework as irrelevant for her goals, her emotional decision will be NO. If it is relevant, she moves on the next question: "Is this new? Did I exoect this?" … and so on.

When Branka introduced me to her model I said "Branka, stop please. This cannot be correct. Look, I work for HP. We bring out one innovation after the other, I see no one rejecting novelty" – "Dieter," she replied, "did you listen to what you just said?" – Point made, I guess.

In the same way, people evaluate the request to deliver a necessary condition. The bigger the change required by such requests, the more likely it is that the emotional decision will be NO. Success or failure of many major changes like re-organizations or mergers are determined by how well management identifies and overcomes emotional, not just physical obstacles.[65]

Identifying emotional obstacles to necessary conditions

The Zei-Pollermann model comes handy to assess emotional obstacles for necessary conditions.

For illustration purposes let us apply this model to a project for applying TOC methodologies like drum-buffer-rope or critical chain project management in a manufacturing site, where these methods are not in use today.

Each person expected to engage in such effort will ask, for herself or himself these four questions:

Is this relevant for my own intentions/goals? Would not know why it would be.

Is this new? Did I expect this? Totally new, perhaps just another one of these new management models (which will go away, when they discover the next one, anyway).

Can I cope with its consequences? No. Neither am I competent in TOC, nor can I estimate the possible consequences.

Is this in agreement with social norms? Do others do it? Yes, company XYZ – but that is not our industry. Nobody in our company does it.

---

[65] http://www.globoforce.com/gfblog/2012/6-big-mergers-that-were-killed-by-culture/

Three rules for defining right obstacles

When searching for obstacles the *intuitive System 1* jumps to conclusions, presenting convincing obstacles in an instant. Too often, obstacles found that way are just recalled from anecdotes. Obstacles presented with "of course" or "as we all know" should make us suspicious and send us running to double check using *data-driven System 2*.

Obstacle to increasing sales productivity? – The commission scheme of course. Obstacle to improving on time delivery? The factory is unreliable, as we all know. Obstacle to success of new products? It's obvious that our sales force is incompetent. Data needed, please.

1. Operationalize obstacles

To operationalize obstacles, define the function where they appear and the operational performance gap. (See examples in Fig.10.4)

Necessary condition	Obstacles	
	Intuitive (System 1)	Data based (System 2)
95% on-time customer acceptance	We are not competent enough to quickly install.	In Service, we need 25 technicians trained. Only 18 are trained now.
< 6 months for new products	We take too long to develop new products	In Product Development, we need manufacturing release after 6 months of development. Currently, 3 of 10 projects take more than 6 months.
120 m$ level of qualified funnel	We do not generate enough leads	In Sales, we require $300 M in new leads per quarter. Marketing currently generates $225 M
< 8 % marketing cost envelope	We have too many product options and our win rate is too low.	In Product Development, we have 98 product options, should have max. 5
		In Sales, our opportunity win rate is <30%, should be > 50%

Figure 10.4 Obstacles, operationalized as performance gaps
Intuitive phrasing needs to be operationalized into data-based description of the gap of which the obstacle consists.

In the extreme case a function may be required, but missing. Then the absence of the function is the obstacle. "We need a dealer network, but don't have one".

One obstacle per statement

Intuitive descriptions of obstacles often mix several obstacles into one phrase. If an obstacle contains words like AND, OR or BOTH the statement contains several obstacles. In order to operationalize correctly, make sure that each statement describes only one obstacle. "We have too many product options and our win rate is too low" includes two obstacles, which appear in two different functions and thus would each need different approaches to removing them.

2. Check the entire business system

There is no man more pusillanimous than I when I am planning a campaign. I purposely exaggerate all the dangers and all the calamities that the circumstances make possible. Napoleon Bonaparte

The bigger the change required by the necessary condition, the more functions might contain obstacles and thus the bigger the risk of overlooking some. To avoid the WYSIATI (what you see is all there is) trap, search the entire business system – function by function - for obstacles to each necessary condition. The worksheet provided later in this chapter can be used as an obstacle search grid to support this systematic search.

3. Consider emotional obstacles

Not only will more change bring forward more obstacles – it will also make it more likely that emotional obstacles surface. Don't overlook these; check each necessary condition for potential emotional obstacles.

Worksheet and operational plan

Use a worksheet as before to check the entire system for obstacles.

Note, that we are following the rules for "right obstacles": they are phrased as performance gaps and contain one obstacle per statement, related to one function of the business system. The example shows both physical and emotional obstacles.

When completed, transfer search results to the one page plan, which is now close to completion.

Cultural domain	Ecosystem			Internal System					Necessary conditions
	Suppliers	Enablers	Customers	Op. Leadership Edward E.	Service Thomas T.	Supply Chain William W.	Sales & Mktg Mary M.	Products James T.	
Our culture does not value engineering efficiency								We should manage development as projects, don't do that.	1.1 Product development: < 6 months new product cycle James T. BT (01-16)
					We do not track TTF as KPI, should have accountable owner				1.2 Service: > 8 hours time to fix Thomas T. IP (03-16)
Engineering efficiency is a new performance indicator								We have up to 98 options per product, should have max 5	2.1 Marketing: +15% RFQs by web marketing Mary M. BT (12-15)
				We lack an agreed upon key account approach, should have one for all functions.			Key account opportunity win rate is <30%, should be > 50%		2.2 Sales: $60m key account sales Frank F. IP (FY-16)
								Nr of parts is > 20,000 should be < 2000	3.1 Manufacturing: < $25m COGS Edward E. IP (12-15)
					Excess/obsolency is 19% should be < 12%				3.2 Supply chain inventory driven cost < 14% of revenue William W. IP (03-16)
Separating and focusing on PLs is unpleasant for managers							Staff sells product mix, should sell only PL A or B		4.1 Co-management Separate organizations for value chains of PL A and B Edward E. BT (07-15)

Figure 10.5 Worksheet obstacle search grid
Checking every single function of the business system for obstacles to achieving necessary conditions. The business ecosystem is check in entirety. Check includes the cultural domain.

Commitments	Obstacles	Necessary conditions	Competitors' plans	Critical success factors	Operational business goal
	We should manage development as projects, don't do that presently	1.1 Product development: < 6 months new product cycle James T. BT (01-2016)	(A) Perf.Goal: Stable product development cycle > 12 mths, ongoing	1. Advantage in trends in user needs	
	Our culture does not value engineering efficiency				
	We do not track TTF as KPI, should have accountable owner	1.2 Service: > 8 hours time to fix Thomas T. IP (03-16)	(B) Perf.Goal: Top service rating > TTF < 3 days (ongoing) > 65% parts on stock (12-15)		
	We have up to 98 options per product, should have max 5	2.1 Marketing: +15% RFQs by web marketing Mary M. BT (12-15)	(B) Perf. Goal: $8m sales/head >50/50 incentive scheme >Sales work from home Both ongoing	2. Highly effective sales function	Contribution margin 2015: $250m 2016: $280m
	Key account opportunity win rate is <30%, should be > 50%	2.2 Sales: $60m key account sales Frank F. JP (FY-16)			
	We lack an agreed upon key account approach, should have one for all functions.				
	Nr of parts is > 20.000 should be < 2000	3.1 Manufacturing: < $25m COGS Edward E. EP (12-15)	(A) Perf. Goal: Cost of material < 15% > New supplier contracts (12-15)	3. World class low cost organization	
	Cost of warranty is 19%, should be < 5%	3.2 Supply chain: Inventory driven cost < 14% of revenue William W. IP (03-16)	(B): Perf. Goal: Final configuration ex works > Customer config via Web (06-15)		
	Staff sells product mix, should sell only PL A or B	4.1 Company management: Separate organizations for value chains of PL A and B Edward E. BT (07-15)	(A),(B) Perf. Goal: Profit by country, ongoing. No plans for separate units by product lines.	4. Highly focused product line teams	
	Separating and focusing on PLs is unpleasant for managers				

Figure 10.6 Designing the operational plan – Step 4: Note obstacles for necessary conditions
One or more obstacles for NCs logged in the one-page plan.

Chapter 11: Commitments

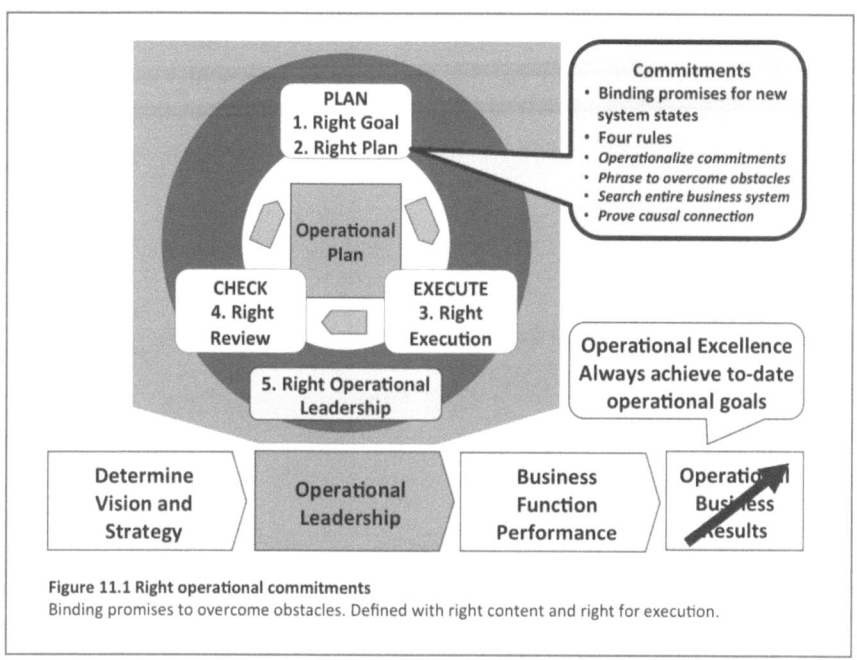

Figure 11.1 Right operational commitments
Binding promises to overcome obstacles. Defined with right content and right for execution.

Obstacles won't just go away by themselves. Specific action is required to achieve system states through which they will be overcome.

Traditionally such states are called objectives. In operational plans however, this term does not accurately get to the heart of the matter.

Lukewarm "will try to do my best" objectives are not helpful. Instead you need to require unconditional, firm, irrevocable and binding commitment by single accountable owners to lead the business system to the state of performance such that the obstacle is resolved.

To do so, follow four rules to establish right commitments in the plan.

Operational commitments: Promises for new system states

States to be achieved

In the example in Figure 11.2, the obstacle for growing sales is found in selling to key accounts. In this company, sales people have traditionally been technical experts. But now customers have changed. They do not want to be told about product features. Instead, they want to compare offers based on their business value. To address this customer requirement the sales people must be competent in value-based selling, which they are not.

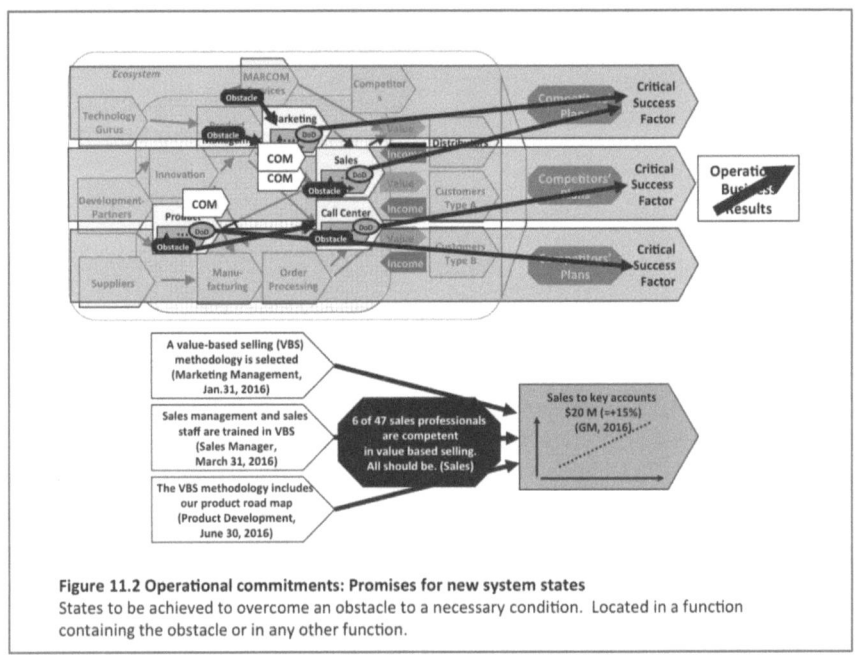

Figure 11.2 Operational commitments: Promises for new system states
States to be achieved to overcome an obstacle to a necessary condition. Located in a function containing the obstacle or in any other function.

Three functions need to contribute to overcoming this obstacle. Marketing needs to select one of the value-based selling approaches available, Sales Management needs to lead to ensure that everyone has attended training and Product Development must provide product road maps, which are essential elements of value-based selling.

Binding promises

While necessary conditions are the goals of key operational projects, commitments are their building blocks. We must be able to rely on the robustness of these smallest elements of our surfboard. Each commitment must be a binding promise given unconditionally by its owner.

Four rules for establishing right commitments

1. Operationalize commitments

Phrase commitments as DoDs (Definition of Done)

Each commitment needs to contain one single DoD to be achieved - not an intention.

State single DoDs for each commitment

If a commitment contains the word AND shows we should separate such multiple DoDs into single ones.

Assign commitments to single accountable owners

As for any operational obligation the rule of single accountable ownership applies.

Address emotional obstacles

The advantage of the Zei-Pollermann model is, that it shows clearly the actions required to address an emotional obstacle:

Not relevant for people's goals? Explain why this is, and how they will benefit personally. Not expected? Ensure full communication. Cannot cope? Coach and train. Nobody else does it? Position the business unit as a front runner.

Define due dates

A firm commitment not only promises the DoD (Defintion of Done) but also the date or time by which it will be delivered.

Set milestones for commitments

To prepare to lead delivery we set two kinds of milestones for commitments:

- *DoD milestones* to prepare tracking progress in the commitment's DoD, as described earlier for NCs. These should be set for each period at which progress in the plan will be checked.
- *Building milestones* to prepare tracking progress in creating the prerequisites for delivering the commitment. Develop these by identifying obstacles to the commitment's DoD, and work backwards from there.

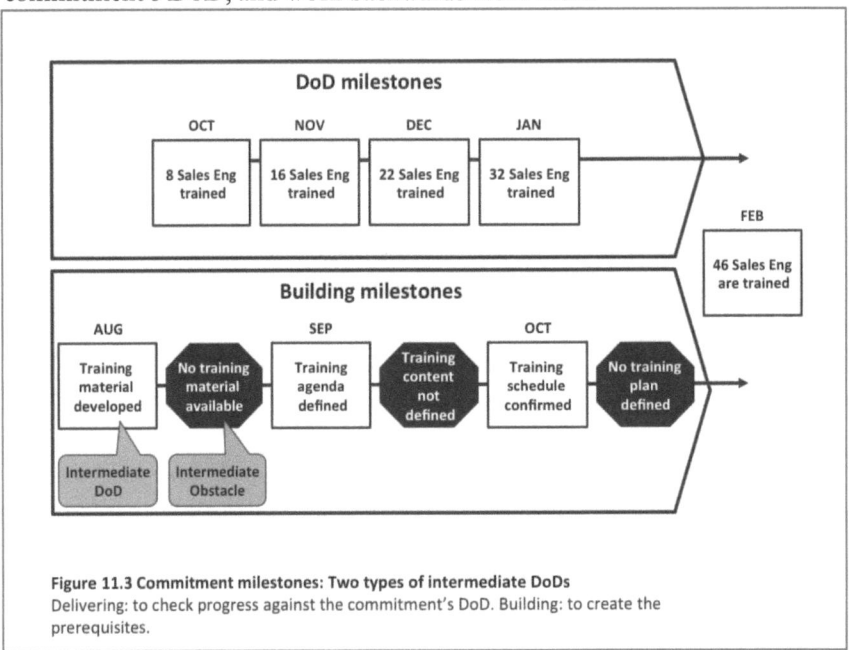

Figure 11.3 Commitment milestones: Two types of intermediate DoDs
Delivering: to check progress against the commitment's DoD. Building: to create the prerequisites.

The more change required by a commitment the denser the building milestones should be. For commitments requiring breakthrough in performance, plan step by step how each intermediate obstacle will be overcome.

Chapter 11: Commitments

2. Phrase commitments to overcome obstacles

William Dettmer[66] recommends using the verb overcome, not remove or obliterate, to describe what a commitment should do to an obstacle. Certainly, it can be removed or destroyed by taking action for that purpose. But a way around it might also be discovered, thus making the obstacle irrelevant for the necessary condition.

> *In the late 1990's Hanns-Per Kober, CEO of Tetra Pak Austria was faced with a massive obstacle. The Austrian government was considering a law declaring juice cartons as "non recyclable". As result, a penalty would be charged for every single juice carton placed into the consumption chain. If this obstacle could not be resolved, it would have been the end of his business in Austria for Tetra Pak. (The law would have given a monopoly to glass bottles, since glass was considered fully recyclable).*

Figure 11.4 The eco (German: öko) bag
Showcase example of resolving an obstacle by „going around". (carton box, folded)

---

[66] Dettmer, H. William: The logical thinking process. ASQ Quality Press, Milwaukee, WI. 2007

He resolved the obstacle by "going around it." His company offered, free of charge, an "eco-box" container in which consumers could collect folded juice cartons. If you sent these boxes back to Tetra Pak, you would participate in a lottery. The postage was already paid, so all consumers had to do was bring their boxes to the post office. – Result: 100% of Tetra Pak boxes were recycled, at no charge to the consumer, conforming to the new law.

To completely recycle the returned boxes Hanns-Per Kober found a paper mill that would recycle the returned boxes, so the material could be used as raw material for other purposes.

3. Search the entire business system

Often not just one single function needs to contribute to overcome an obstacle. To avoid the WYSIATI trap again search the entire business system.

4. Prove the causal connection

Require proof for the causal connection between an obstacle and its commitments in form of data. For our example, we need data proving that:

- Sales professionals with higher competence in value-based selling actually sell more,
- Training in value-based selling will result in higher competence, and
- Product road maps are essential for convincing customers of the value offered.

Worksheet and operational plan

For searching the entire business system a worksheet is again valuable. When the search is done the operational plan can be completed

Chapter 11: Commitments

Ecosystem			Commitments to overcome obstacles					Obstacles	Necessary conditions
Suppliers	Enablers	Customers	Op. Leadership Edward E.	Service Thomas T.	Internal System Supply Chain William W.	Sales & Mktg Mary M.	Products James T.		
			Engineering efficiency workshop all engineers (02-15)				CCPM in use for new products (05-15)	We should manage development as projects, do that presently	1.1 Product development: < 6 months new product cycle James T. BT (01-16)
				Service supervisors manage TTF as KPI (06-15)				Our culture does not value engineering efficiency	1.2 Service: > 8 hours time to fix Thomas T. IP (03-16)
						Five options only on price list (10-15)		We have up to 98 product options, per product, should have max 5	2.1 Marketing: +15% RFQs by web marketing Mary M. BT (13-15)
			Must win deals reviewed monthly (04-15)			Deal qualification is revised (05-15)		Key account opportunity win rate is <30%, should be > 50%	2.2 Sales: 560m key account sales Frank F. IP (FY-16)
			Key account approach agreed upon (04-15)		Design for assembly in place for PL A (86-15)			We lack an agreed upon key account approach, should have one for all functions.	
				DOA reduced to < 1% (12-15)				Nr of parts is > 20.000 should be < 2000	3.1 Manufacturing: < 525m COGS Edward E. IP (12-15)
						Revised sales contracts signed (06-15)		Cost of warranty is 19%, should be < 5%	3.2 Supply chain: Inventory driven cost < 14% of revenue William W. IP (03-16)
		Customers informed of focused staff (03-15)	Engagement workshops with managers (02-15)					Staff sells product mix, should sell only PL A or B	4.1 Separate organisations for value chains of PL A and B Edward E. BT (07-15)
								Separating and focusing on PLs is unpleasant for managers	

Figure 11.5 Defining commitments – Worksheet (Example)
Searching the entire business system for commitments required to overcome obstacles to necessary commitments.

Chapter 11: Commitments

Commitments	Obstacles	Necessary conditions	Competitors' plans	Critical success factors	Operational business goal
Critical chain project management in use for new products James T. (05-15)	We should manage development as projects, don't do that presently	1.1 Product development: < 6 months new product cycle James T. BT (01-2016)	(A) Perf. Goal: Stable product development cycle > 12 mths, ongoing	1. Advantage in trends in user needs	Contribution margin 2015: $250m 2016: $280m
All engineers attended engineering efficiency workshop Edward E. (02-15)	Our culture does not value engineering efficiency				
Service supervisors manage TTF as KPI, Thomas T. (06-15)	We do not track TTF as KPI, should have accountable owner	1.2 Service: > 8 hours time to fix Thomas T. IP (03-16)	(B) Perf. Goal: Top service rating > TTF < 3 days (ongoing) > 65% parts on stock (12-15)		
Five options only on price list Mary M. (10-15)	We have up to 98 options per product, should have max 5	2.1 Marketing: +15% RFQs by web marketing Mary M. BT (12-15)		2. Highly effective sales function	
Deal qualification is revised Mary M. (05-15)	Key account opportunity win rate is <30%, should be > 50%	2.2 Sales: $60m key account sales Frank E. IP (FY-16)	(B) Perf. Goal: $8m sales/head >50/50 incentive scheme >Sales work from home Both ongoing		
Must win deals are reviewed monthly Edward E. (04-15)					
Key account approach agreed upon Edward E. (04-15)	We lack an agreed upon key account approach, should have one for all functions.				
Design for assembly in place for PL A William W. (06-15)	Nr of parts is > 20.000 should be < 2000	3.1 Manufacturing: < $m 550 COGS Edward E. IP (12-15)	(A) Perf. Goal: Cost of material < 15% > New supplier contracts (12-15)	3. World class low cost organization	
DOA reduced to < 1% Thomas T. (12-15)	Cost of warranty is 19%, should be < 5%	3.2 Supply chain: < $285m total cost of supply chain William W. IP (03-16)	(B) Perf. Goal: Final configuration ex works > Customer config via Web (06-15)		
Revised sales contracts signed Mary M. (06-15)	Staff sells product mix, should sell only PL A or B	4.1 Company management: Separate organisations for value chains of PL A and B Edward E. BT (07-15)	(A),(B) Perf. Goal: Profit by country, ongoing. No plans for separate units by product lines.	4. Highly focused product line teams	
Customers informed of focused staff Mary M. (03-15)					
Engagement workshops with managers Edward E. (02-15)	Separating and focussing on PLs is unpleasant for managers				

Figure 11.6 Completing the operational plan – Step 5: Noting commitments for overcoming obstacles
Upon entering the commitments, the one-page plan is completed.

Chapter 12: All obligations confirmed

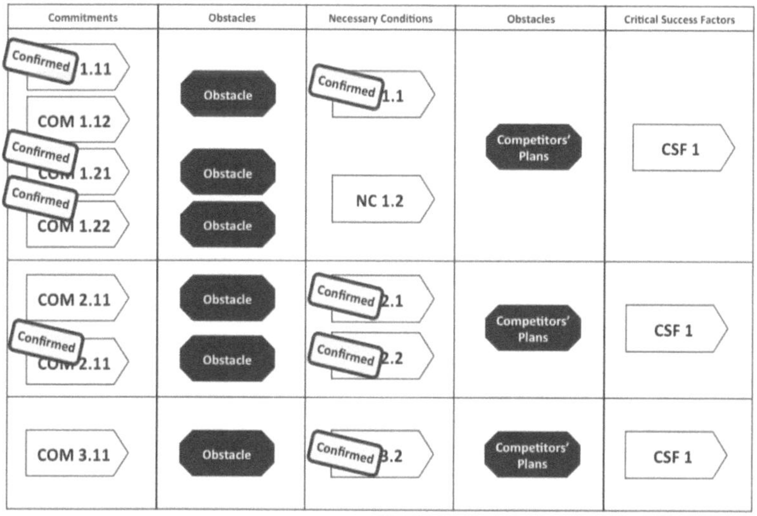

Figure 12.1 All obligations must be confirmed – otherwise, the operational plan is incomplete
By confirming obligations, owners accept accountability to deliver the obligations' DoDs.

The best way to keep one's word is not to give it. Napoleon Bonaparte

This is the shortest chapter in the book. But it is vital.

In the euphoria of planning workshops we are often tempted to promise too much. But: will it get done? Before declaring the plan finished, all owners of obligations must double-check their obligations. Are the DoDs of necessary conditions, commitments and milestones clear and feasible? Are the required resources available? YES? Only then each obligation can be confirmed.

As long as one single obligation is unconfirmed, the operational plan is not completed, the surfboard not yet glued together.

Chapter 13: Right execution

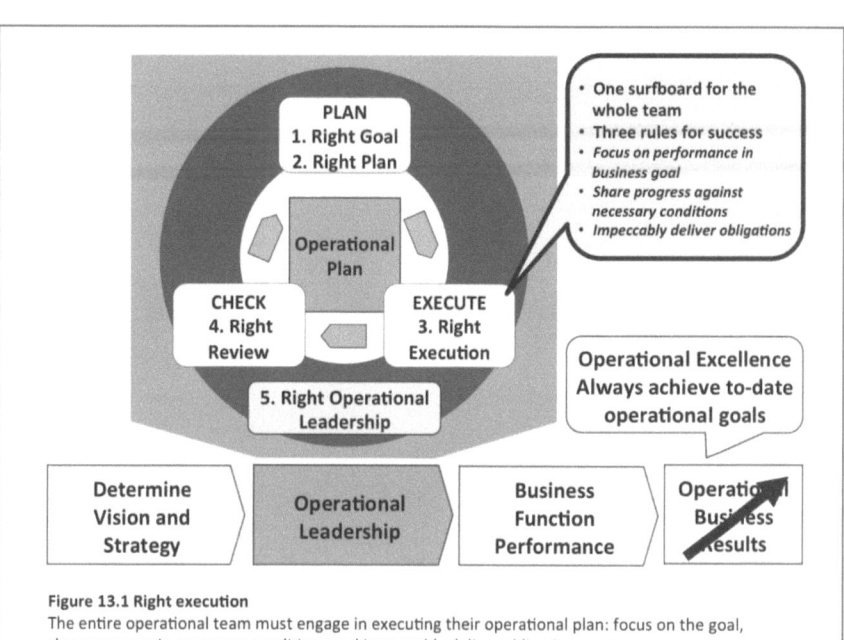

Figure 13.1 Right execution
The entire operational team must engage in executing their operational plan: focus on the goal, share progress in necessary conditions and impeccably deliver obligations.

You selected the wave to ride, set the operational goals and built the perfect surfboard, the operational plan. So far, this was work for your grey cells.

Now let's go surfing and ride the wave! Let's execute the plan.

The goal chart is ready to steer you. The operational plan is simple, focused on the essentials and ready for execution.

This is not surfing as usual. It's the entire operational team surfing on one board. Everyone in the operational team must fulfill three tasks to ensure right execution of the plan.

The entire operational team on one surfboard

It's not just the operational leader surfing. It's the entire operational team on one board, the operational plan.

Figure 13.2 Executing operational plans: the entire operational team on one surfboard
Everyone must focus on the goal and contribute as committed.

On this surfboard every team member must fulfill three tasks: focus on the operational goal and on necessary conditions and flawlessly deliver against obligations.

1. Focus attention on the operational business goal

An up-to-date copy of the team's goal chart must always be available. Figure 13.3 shows the essential features of such goal charts:
- Clear. Only shows the one operational business goal. (Chapter 4, Right goals).
- Shows progress at the top level and (if established) for next lower level business units.
- Presents the forecast.
- Comments on results (explaining the past) and forecast (foreseeing constraints)

Chapter 13: Right execution

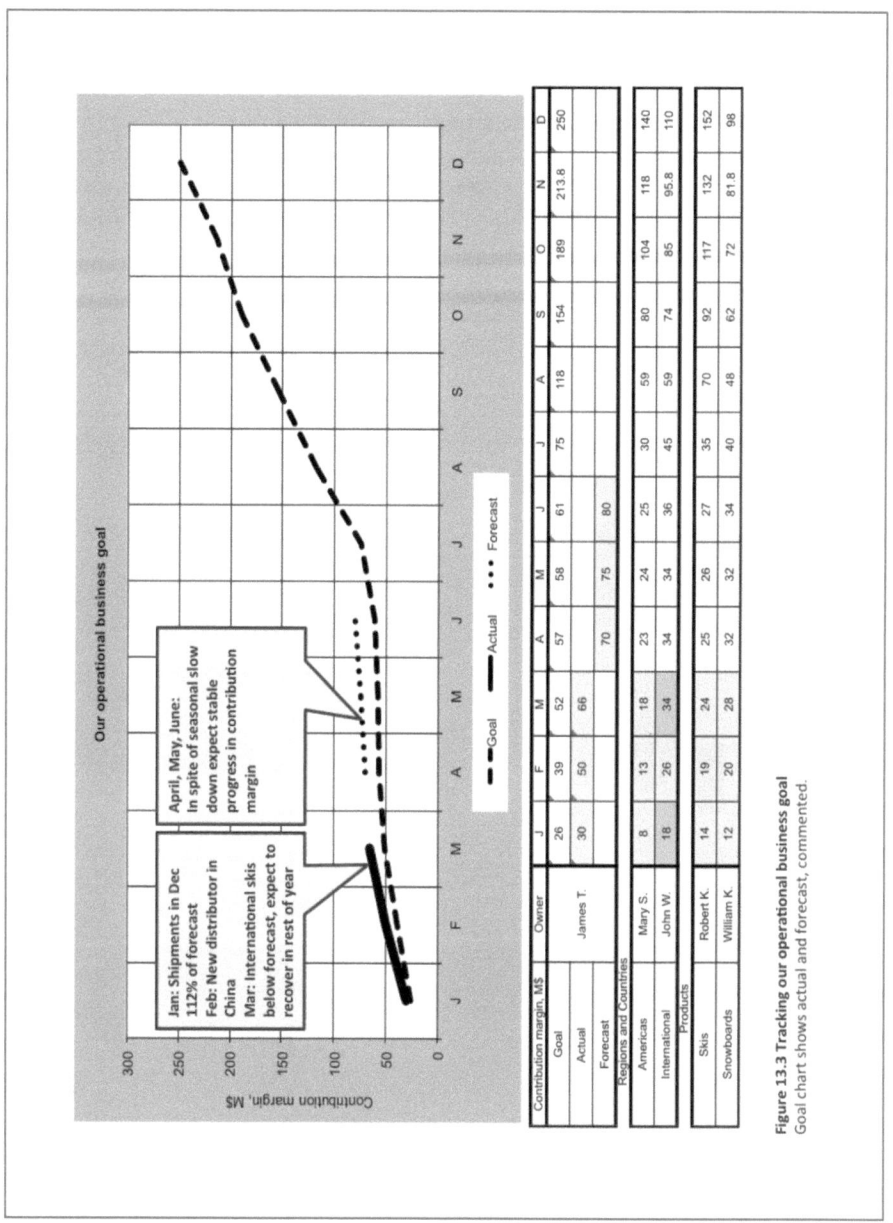

Figure 13.3 Tracking our operational business goal
Goal chart shows actual and forecast, commented.

Chapter 13: Right execution

2. Track progress toward necessary conditions

Necessary conditions are the "must achieve" DoDs (Definition of Done) of key operational projects. To track progress toward achieving NCs is mandatory. Such progress confirms that the right obstacles have been identified and are being successfully resolved. Owners of NCs must keep team members updated on their progress. Everyone on the team must always have a full view of progress in the entire operational plan.

Track progress on NCs for the entire plan

To share progress on all NC's of one plan a summarizing tracking table is helpful.

Progress in necessary conditions												Necessary conditions	Competitors' plans	Critical success factors	Operational business goal
Jan	Feb	Mar	Apr	May	Jun	Jul	Aug	Sep	Oct	Nov	Dec				
												1.1 Product development: < 6 months new product cycle James T. BT (01-2016)	(A) Perf.Goal: Stable product development cycle > 12 mths, ongoing	1. Advantage in trends in user needs	
		OFF TR	OFF TR	OFF TR								1.2 Service: > 8 hours time to fix Thomas T. IP (03-16)	(B) Perf.Goal: Top service rating > TTF < 3 days (ongoing) > 65% parts on stock (12-15)		
												2.1 Marketing: +15% RFQs by web marketing Mary M. BT (12-15)	(B) Perf. Goal: $8m sales/head >50/50 incentive scheme >Sales work from home Both ongoing	2. Highly effective sales function	Contribution margin 2015: $250m 2016: $280m
OFF TR	OFF TR	OFF TR										2.2 Sales: $60m key account sales Frank F. IP (FY-16)			
		OFF TR			OFF TR							3.1 Manufacturing: < $m 550 COGS Edward E. IP (12-15)	(A) Perf.Goal: Cost of material < 15% > New supplier contracts (12-15)	3. World class low cost organization	
												3.2 Supply chain: < $285m total cost of supply chain William W. IP (03-16)	(B) Perf.Goal: Final configuration ex works > Customer config via Web (06-15)		
OFF TR	OFF TR	OFF TR	OFF TR	OFF TR								4.1 Company management: Separate organizations for value chains of PL A and B Edward E. BT (07-15)	(A),(B) Perf.Goal: Profit by country, ongoing. No plans for separate units by product lines.	4. Highly focused product line teams	

Figure 13.4 Tracking progress in necessary conditions. Summary for operational plan
Progress against all necessary conditions, by their milestones.

Color coding "on track" or "off track" makes it easy to understand the situation at a glance. For clarity, there is no "amber" indicator. Either you are on or off track.

Track each NC's progress against its DoD

A good practice is to follow each NC using a specific goal chart, as shown in the illustration. NCs can only be tracked in this way if they have been operationalized as described in Chapter 9 (Necessary conditions).

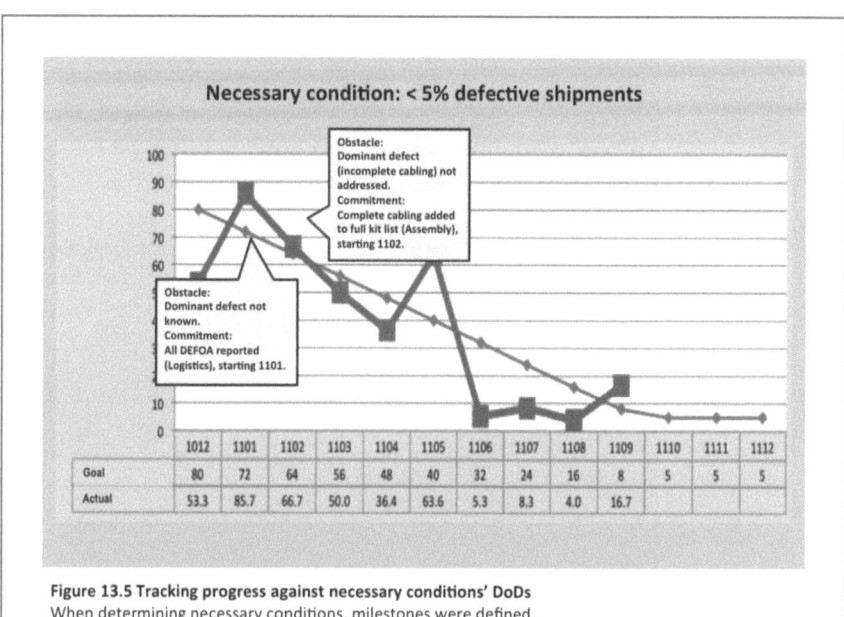

Figure 13.5 Tracking progress against necessary conditions' DoDs
When determining necessary conditions, milestones were defined. Based on these, track and share progress.

3. Flawlessly deliver against obligations

I am invariably late for appointments – sometimes as much as two hours. I've tried to change my ways but the things that make me late are too strong, and too pleasing.
Marilyn Monroe

There are many reasons why people struggle to keep promises. We just forget what we promised. (We are not organized to remember what we promised). We shy away from the extra effort. (To be reliable takes extra effort to remember, to prepare, to work on delivery). We don't want to be bound. (A promise binds us, reduces our personal freedom. We don't enjoy that.)

The dominant cause of failing in operational execution

Data on why operational plans fail show that low reliability – failure to deliver obligations on time or delivering them incomplete - is the dominant cause.

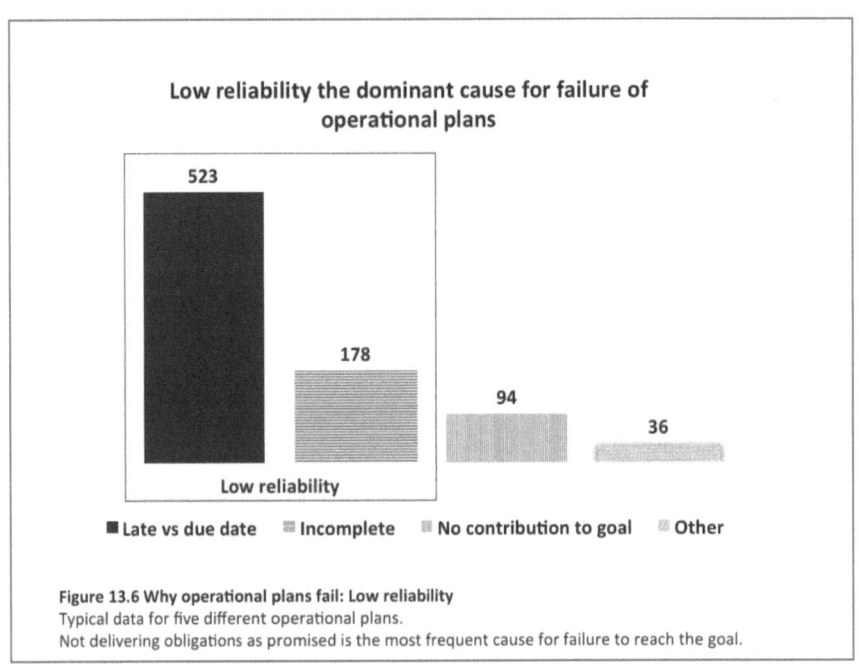

Figure 13.6 Why operational plans fail: Low reliability
Typical data for five different operational plans.
Not delivering obligations as promised is the most frequent cause for failure to reach the goal.

The answer: Flawlessly manage personal obligations

Everyone on the operational team, including leaders, needs to follow an impeccable routine of managing their obligations. After obligations are defined and assigned, the owners must follow the process described below, relentlessly and step by step:

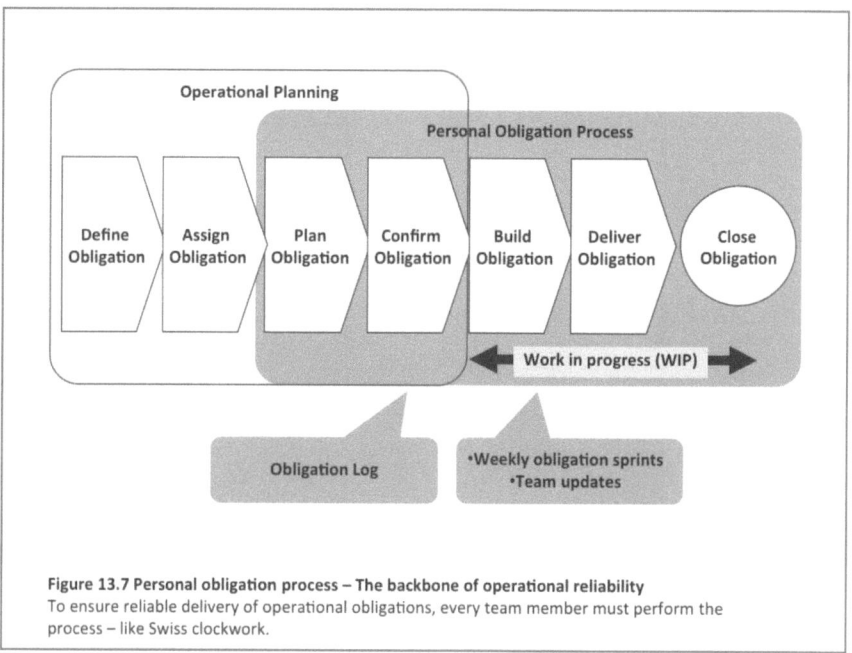

Figure 13.7 Personal obligation process – The backbone of operational reliability
To ensure reliable delivery of operational obligations, every team member must perform the process – like Swiss clockwork.

- Plan. Design the steps to deliver the obligation.
- Confirm. After a workable plan is found, confirm the promise to deliver.
- Log obligations. The centerpiece of managing personal obligations is the owner's obligation log. Whenever owners give a promise, they must note it. This is not an entry in an agenda, but a separate list.
- Work in weekly obligation sprints. Plan your week around the obligation(s) you are delivering.
- Update the operational team. Owners must keep the entire operational team updated on progress against goals and obligations. If unexpected obstacles appear owners MUST report back.

- Deliver. To deliver an obligation means to achieve the DoD promised. Obligation owners must check whether they actually achieved the DoD they promised.
- Close. When obligation owners deliver an obligation, they must close it with a short message to the person(s) expecting delivery, thus taking the obligation off of the *open* list. Owners must close obligations without being asked. "Oh, yes, I forgot to tell you. It is done." is not an acceptable practice.

Chapter 14: Right check

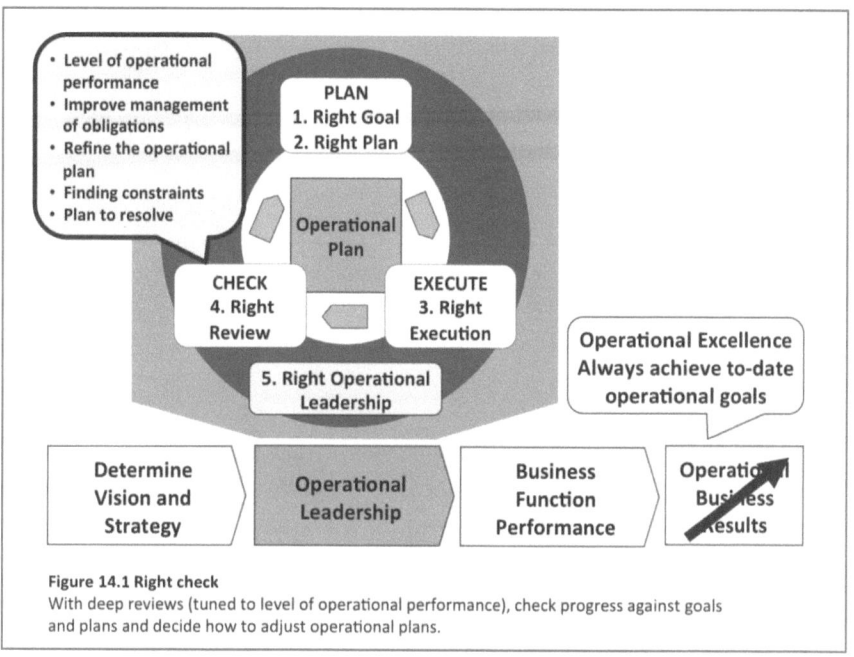

Figure 14.1 Right check
With deep reviews (tuned to level of operational performance), check progress against goals and plans and decide how to adjust operational plans.

An operational sprint has been completed. Time to check if we are doing the right things right.

We want to find the bad news: Where was our surfing not perfect? How well did we achieve the goals and execute the plans?

The answers to these two questions tell how to adjust or rebuild the operational plan.

Improve delivery of obligations? Leave the plan as it is? Fine-tune it? Rebuild it from scratch? Go deeper and find the constraint limiting our business systems performance?

Deep reviews – tuned to the level of operational performance

Meetings to review operational results and plans can be most frustrating and a waste of time. Either they are dog-and-pony shows where everyone presents how well they did without getting to the heart of the matter. Or they are heated "blame everyone else" sessions.

The agile approach offers a better solution: sprint reviews. The purpose of such reviews is twofold: (a) Understand what was achieved and (b) how we can improve in the future. Thus, they are effective, goal oriented and therefore a pleasure to attend..

Operational performance has two dimensions:

1. How well did we achieve our operational business goals? and
2. How well did we deliver against the operational plan?

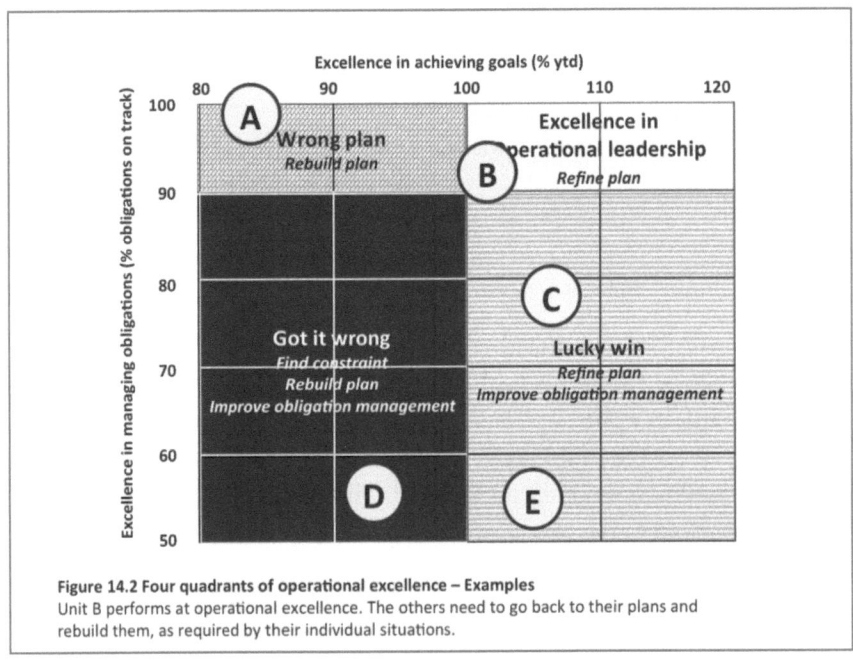

Figure 14.2 Four quadrants of operational excellence – Examples
Unit B performs at operational excellence. The others need to go back to their plans and rebuild them, as required by their individual situations.

The answers position us in one of four quadrants of operational excellence, determining the actions to take. (Figure 14.2)

Excellence in operational leadership quadrant

The goal was achieved in the past and forecasts so indicate it will continue to be achieved. The operational plan contained the right elements and they were well executed. (Unit B in Figure 14.2).

In the deep review, focus on refining the operational plan to prepare what should be done next.

How long a deep review will take in this case depends on how well your operational team logged observations on progress against goals and obligations. If they did a good job the team will be well prepared and can do a deep review in half a day.

If, however, logging was weak, time will now be wasted recovering from that – compiling information on what happened, checking for data. In this case, a deep review may take up to a full day.

Lucky win quadrant

The high-risk situation. You got there, but have no clue how. (Units E and C in the illustration). The *intuitive System 1* tells you: "Because you did everything right". The *data-driven System 2* asks: "But what did we do right?" In this case the agenda includes two items:

- Rebuild the plan. Check item by item. Are these the critical success factors needed? Do we understand our competitors? Again, important sources for information about what needs to be improved are the comments logged during the most recent sprints.
- Find out what constrains the obligations pipeline and decide how to resolve it.

In this case to do a good job may require a full day.

Wrong plan quadrant

We executed the operational plan well – still, the goal has not been achieved. (Unit A in our example). Definitely we followed the wrong plan.

Let's take as example Michel Madec's plan, described in Chapter 6 (Right operational plans/HOSHIN plans). The actions were done as planned, but no progress was achieved in the goal:

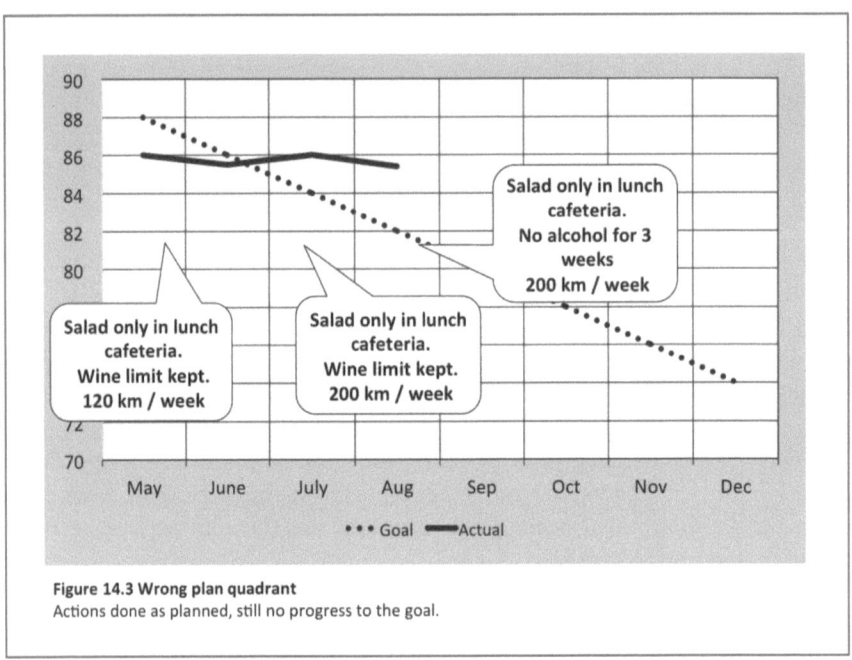

Figure 14.3 Wrong plan quadrant
Actions done as planned, still no progress to the goal.

In such case the deep review focuses on just one thing: rebuild the plan from scratch.

This may take the operational team a full day, sometimes even more.

Got it wrong quadrant

Neither did you achieve the goal, nor did you execute your operational plan. Back to Square One. Unit D in the example.

A unit positioned in this quadrant needs an intensive operational planning session. The result should be an operational plan focused on the core problem - the constraint. The new plan should contain key operational projects for:

- Resolution of the constraint,
- Preventative NC projects,
- Performance of obligations pipeline.

If there is a serious intention to design a 'right' plan, this work may well take two full days.

Improving the management of obligations

The obligation pipeline comprises all obligations in the plan. As owners confirm, build and deliver their obligations these move through the obligation pipeline step by step.

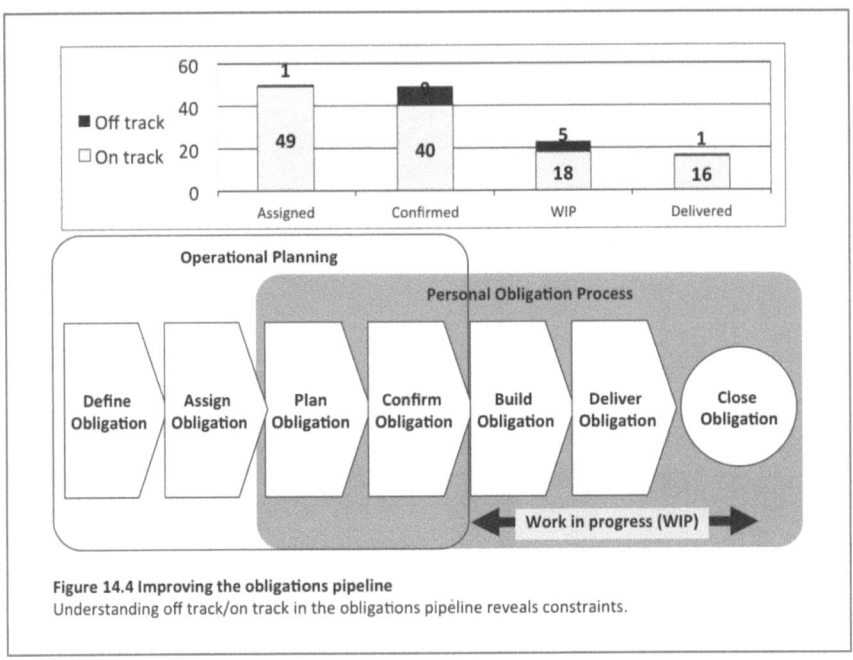

Figure 14.4 Improving the obligations pipeline
Understanding off track/on track in the obligations pipeline reveals constraints.

Data will tell where this pipeline is constrained. In the example in Fig.14.4, two stages in the obligations pipeline are the most constrained:

- The plan is not complete: One of 50 obligations is not assigned and of those assigned 9 have not yet been confirmed.
- We are not reliable: Five of 23 obligations are behind schedule and 1 of 17 were delivered late, a number that will increase, as the owners deliver obligations on which they are working unless we resolve that constraint.

To improve, we need to resolve these bottlenecks.

Refining the operational plan

Refining the content

Sprint reviews in agile software development are a good model for this work. As there, to refine the plan for the next operational sprint, check each of its items with four questions: Stop? Continue? Improve? Or New?

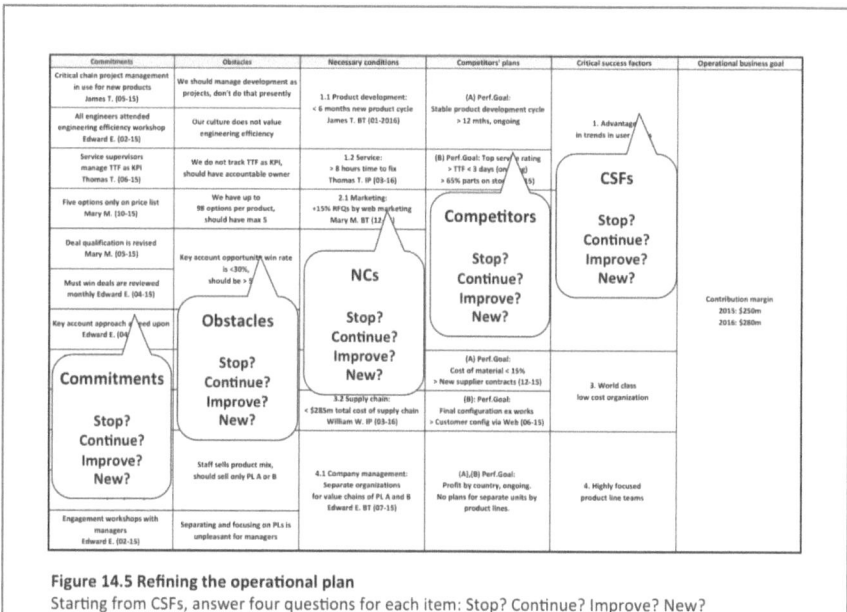

Figure 14.5 Refining the operational plan
Starting from CSFs, answer four questions for each item: Stop? Continue? Improve? New?

Adjusting the structure of operational plan(s)

The deep review is also the opportunity to adjust the structure of the operational plans.

It may be required to add new units, split units up or move them to different positions in the hierarchy. In such cases, adjust your goals accordingly and design new or modify existing operational plans.

Finding constraints in the business system[67]

The goal was missed in spite of perfectly executing the operational plan. A clear signal from our business system: "Friends, I am sick. Your diagnosis was wrong. You must find the true cause of my disease!"

The business system is constrained

Searching for constraints is like diagnosing a sick patient. In traditional Chinese medicine, we would diagnose: "The patient's Chi is blocked somewhere. We need to find the block and resolve it, to reestablish the flow of energy."

Where and what is the constraint? How to dig through the causal network of symptoms to the underlying core problem? When we find it – how to resolve it? For both TOC (theory of constraints) offers powerful tools, the *current reality tree* (CRT) and the *future reality tree* (FRT).

Intensive work for the *data-driven System 2*

Customers were telling us loud and clear: "Your performance in on-time delivery is not acceptable. Either you improve or you are off our supplier list". So we started a project to break through to high reliability in deliveries. One team member said, "Yes, we often miss the delivery dates we commit to customers, but we have no data to understand why we struggle."

Another team member chimed in: "Give me a break with the data stuff. This just results in analysis paralysis. The root cause is obvious. We have known it for years. Our factory in San Jose is always late. All we need is for them to ship on time."

We checked data for on-time shipment from the factory in San Jose. They had addressed the problem one year ago. Now, they shipped >98% on time, every month.

The *intuitive System 1* likes constraints since they provide an opportunity to jump to conclusions. Relying on it when searching for constraints will unfortunately most likely result in a wrong diagnosis missing the constraint. To avoid this mistake the *data-driven System 2* needs to work at full power. To avoid the WYSIATI trap (what you see is all there is), check the business system, function by function. To not jump to conclusions rather operationalize each individual statement for *need* and *have*.

---

[67] For more details on finding constraints with current reality trees (CRTs) see Dettmer, H. William: The Logical Thinking Process. ASQ Quality Press, 2007, p.91 ff.

Two steps to find the constraint

- In a first step, search through the entire business system for causal clusters of symptoms with their consequences and causes.
- In a second step, assemble these clusters into one integrated causal network, in TOC terms the current reality tree (CRT). This core problem resulting in all or most of the symptoms will appear at the bottom of this causal tree.

Finding the constraint, Step 1: Note causal clusters

The tool to use here is a board (wall or flip chart), organized in four columns. In the left-most column note the functions to be analyzed. The three other columns are for noting obstacles, consequences and causes of causal clusters. [68]

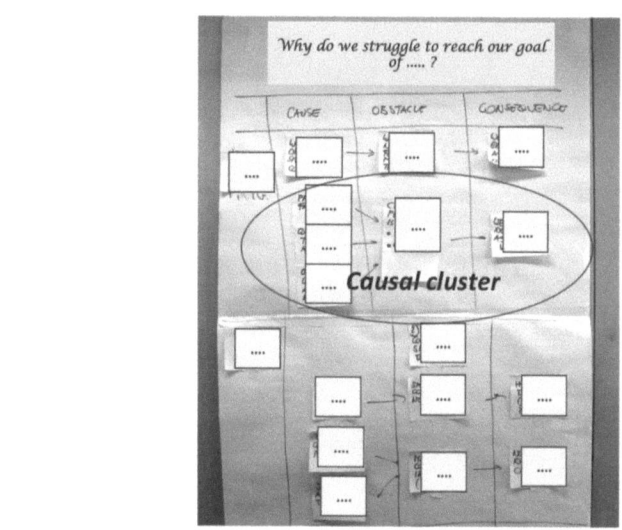

Figure 14.6 Searching for causal clusters: Four column approach
Example. Two functions analyzed. Content covered for confidentiality.

---

[68] This brilliant approach to analyzing problems in logic/causal trees is described in Dettmer, H. William, Breaking the constraints to world class performance. ASQ, 1998. P.83 ff.

The question to answer

Before beginning the search, at the top of the working space note the question to which all observations must relate. This way the *data-driven System 2* can always be called upon to check that the right matters are being discussed.

Note causal clusters

- First check functions in direct contact with customers since they may most directly relate to the undesired effect.
- Use the business system chart to not fall into the WYSIATI trap, checking function by function – for obstacles, consequences and causes.

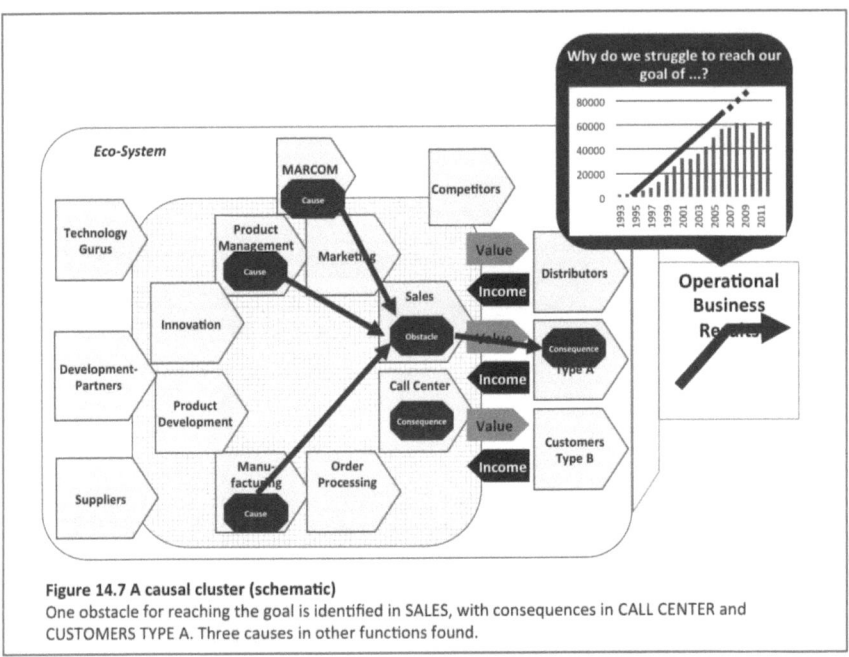

Figure 14.7 A causal cluster (schematic)
One obstacle for reaching the goal is identified in SALES, with consequences in CALL CENTER and CUSTOMERS TYPE A. Three causes in other functions found.

- To build a causal cluster, first note an obstacle that causes the undesired effect (third column from left). Then, identify the consequences for other business functions. Finally, seek its causes within the same or in other functions.
- For each function, repeat these three steps until we find no more obstacles.
- When completed, the entire business system has been checked for causal clusters and it is now time to assemble the CRT.
- During this work, the *data-driven System 2* must be in full action and check each step.

Chapter 14: Right check

Finding the constraint, Step 2: Compile CRT from causal clusters

The CRT (TOC term: current reality tree) rearranges the causal clusters into one integrated causal network, with the constraint at the bottom.

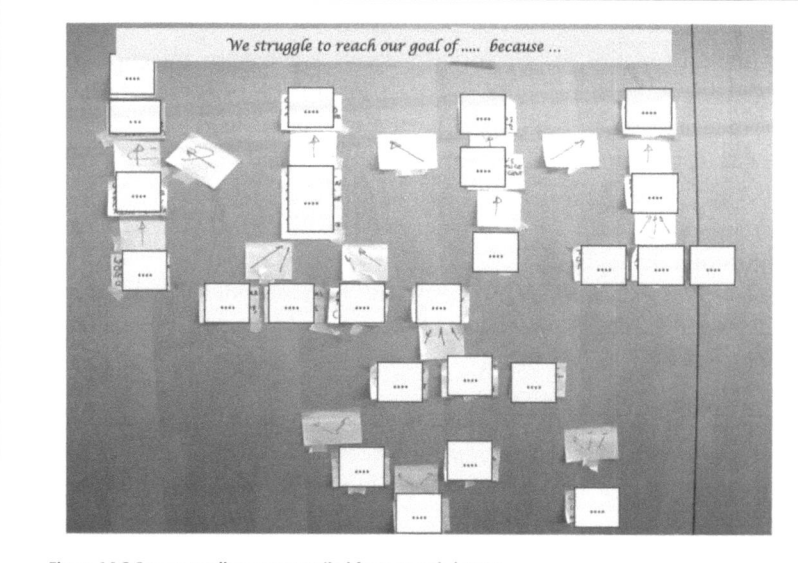

Figure 14.8 Current reality tree compiled from causal clusters
Example. Content covered for confidentially.

- To build it, arrange cluster-by-cluster, working backwards from the undesired effect, connected by arrows indicting causal connection, weaving them into a complete causal network.
- Again, the *data-driven System 2* needs to work full power, rechecking each individual causal connection for correct statement and proof of causality.
- At the bottom of the logic tree, the constraint should now be revealed, the origin of the symptoms resulting in the undesired effect.

Plan to resolve the constraint

To plan resolving the constraint start by defining a DoD that will overcome it. In TOC terms this is an injection into the business system.

Test the plan with a future reality tree (FRT)

It is a good practice to preventively simulate, what the injection will do to your business system before you integrate it into the operational plan. Will it cure the undesired effect (UDE)? Will it cause other effects not related to your purpose of curing the UDE – maybe even unintended negative effects making things worse?[69]

For that test go back to the business system and check the expected effect of the injections throughout it.

To overcome the WYSIATI trap (what you see is all there is) of intuition, again check the effect of the injection function by function throughout the business system.

Add the injection to the operational plan

After that test is completed, add the injection to the operational plan. This can be done either as a key operational project with an NC as DoD, or even as critical success factor.

---

[69] See the law of unintended consequences at
https://en.wikipedia.org/wiki/Unintended_consequences

Chapter 14: Right check

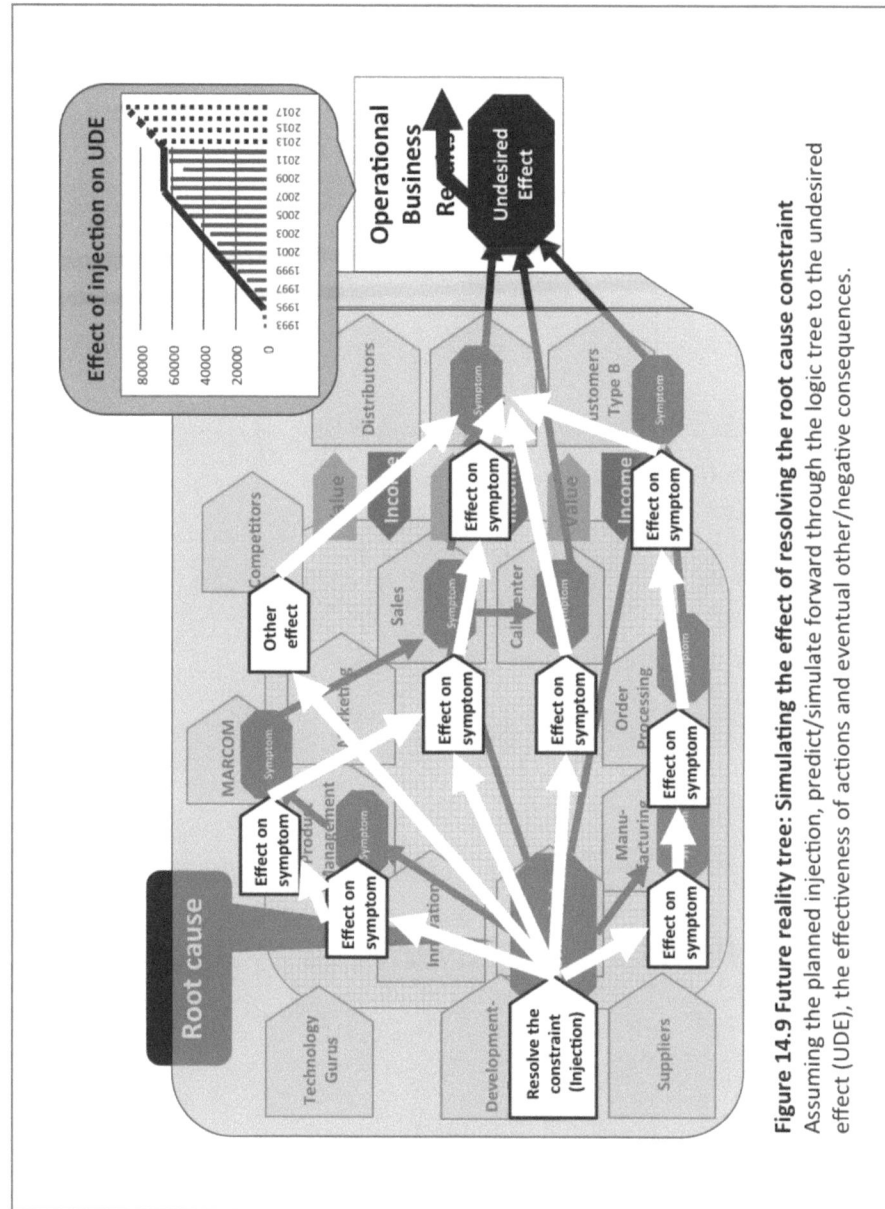

Figure 14.9 Future reality tree: Simulating the effect of resolving the root cause constraint
Assuming the planned injection, predict/simulate forward through the logic tree to the undesired effect (UDE), the effectiveness of actions and eventual other/negative consequences.

Chapter 15: Right operational leadership

The value added by a leader is the difference between what the members of a team can do individually and the result the whole team actually achieves. William (Bill) Russell, Executive VP HP

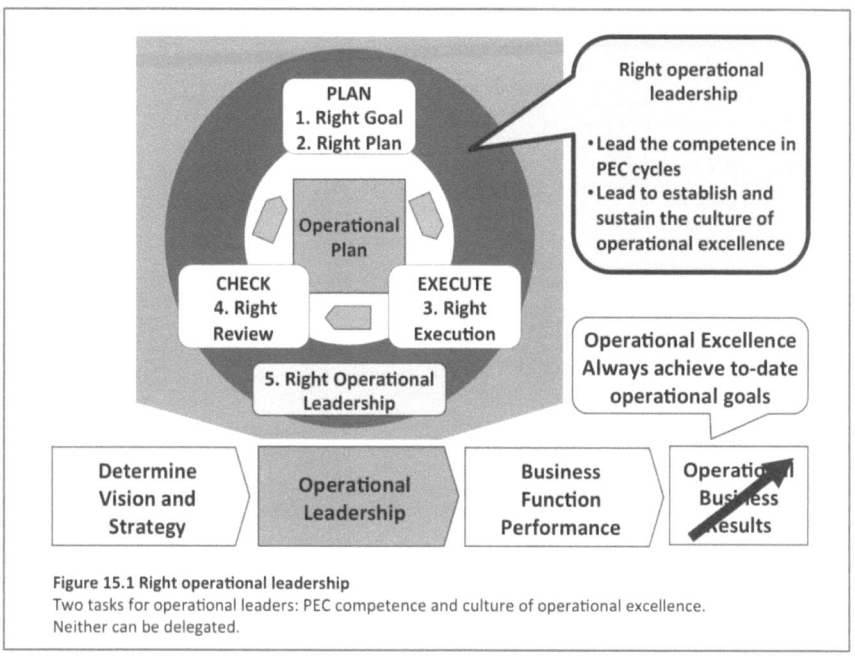

Figure 15.1 Right operational leadership
Two tasks for operational leaders: PEC competence and culture of operational excellence. Neither can be delegated.

Couldn't the operational teams just spin their PEC (Plan-Execute-Check) cycles on their own? Is there any value we add as operational leaders?

You bet there is. Our job as operational leaders comprises two tasks that only we can do: Lead performance of the PEC cycles and develop and sustain a culture of operational excellence.

The business system will never reach operational excellence if we fail to fulfill this duty. This duty cannot be delegated.

Leading our PEC cycles: Four leadership events

Four key events make up the process for leading the performance of PEC (Plan-Execute-Check) cycles:

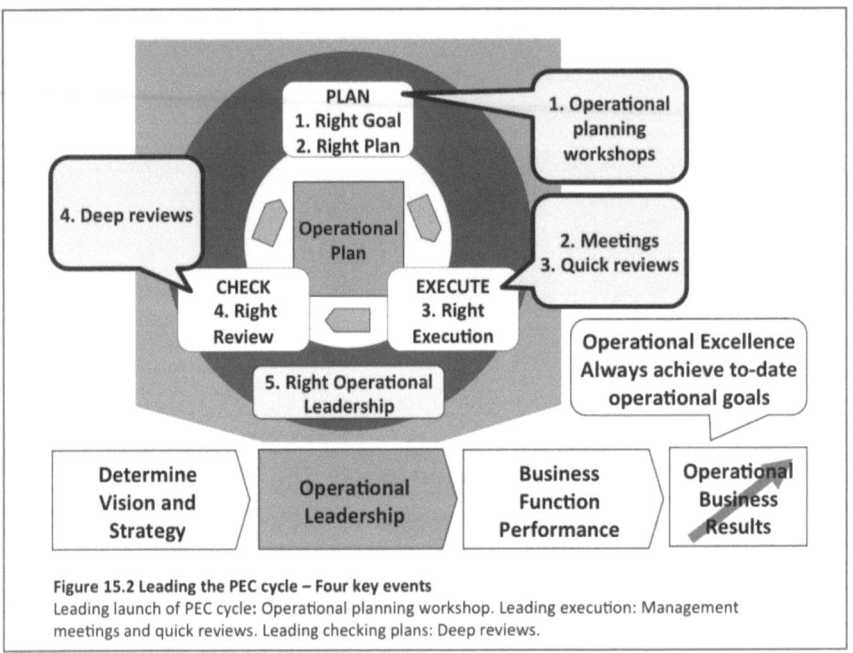

Figure 15.2 Leading the PEC cycle – Four key events
Leading launch of PEC cycle: Operational planning workshop. Leading execution: Management meetings and quick reviews. Leading checking plans: Deep reviews.

- Operational planning workshops: In these workshops you launch the use of PEC cycles or rebuild your operational plan(s) as result of deep reviews.
- Meetings: Every meeting you attend - independent of the participants - is an opportunity to lead focus on the operational goal and on delivery of obligations, and especially of the plan's necessary conditions.
- Quick reviews: In these operational sprint standup meetings, lead the execution of the operational plan(s).
- Deep reviews: In these events, critically review your progress against the goal and plan(s). Then decide how to move forward or adjust/improve.

Leading key event No.1: The operational planning workshop

Kick-off event for PEC cycles

The most effective way to launch PEC cycles is to organize a workshop in which the first operational plan is developed. At the same time you should use this opportunity to coach the operational team in the methodology.

Rebuilding operational plans

When in a deep review you have decided to rebuild the operational plan use the same workshop.

Figure 15.3 The operational planning workshop
Work space with system diagram on the left and operational plans to the right.

A stand-up workshop

A good practice is to do that work standing up, with working space on the wall. For the elements of the plan, use sticky notes, which allows flexibility in designing the causal network of the plan. It is also a good way for teams to visualize the plan as "their piece of art."

Workshops for several company business units

Sometimes it may be necessary to design the plans for several of your business units at one time. In that case – for example, for product lines – the workshop can include several units in one session.

Perfectly prepared

In preparing for the operational planning workshop, be sure to have the necessary strategic information available: the roles, responsibilities and goals of units; triggers and waves expected; expectations of customers and channels; competitors' operational performance and speed; products and services planned and performance data of your key functions.[70]

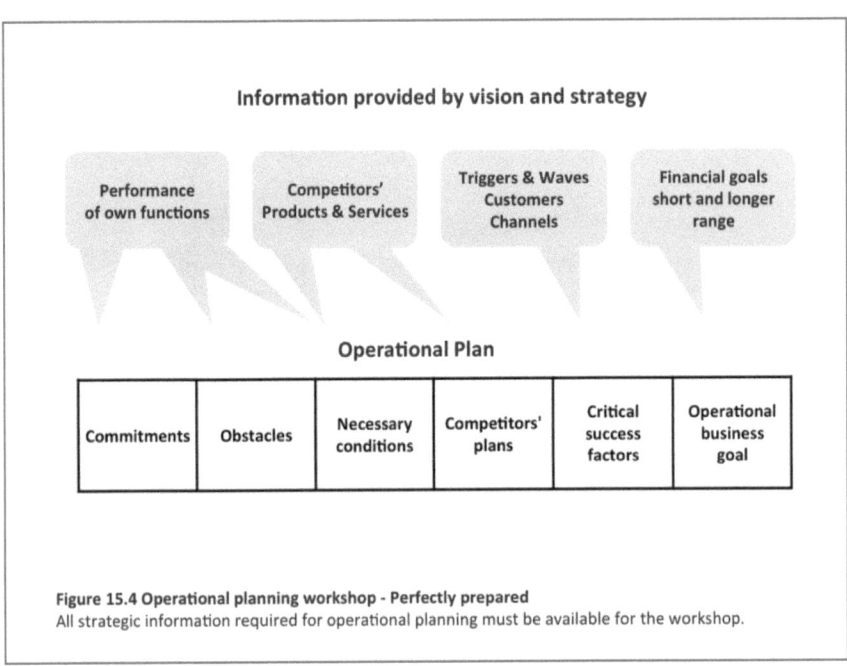

Figure 15.4 Operational planning workshop - Perfectly prepared
All strategic information required for operational planning must be available for the workshop.

---

[70] Also see Chapter 1 on information required from strategies.

Light or full version

It can take two days and intensive effort using the *data-driven System 2* to design an operational plan. Often, inexperienced teams are already exhausted after the first day.

To cope, start with a light version, developing the information required as a minimum for arriving at a good-enough operational plan. Later, for instance at the next deep review, it can be fleshed out and refined.

Element	Light version: Good Enough	Full version: Right
Goal chart	Income goal, linear	Income goal, with seasonality
System diagram	Key functions with owners Added value as comment For multiple business units, one common system diagram	More than key functions Added value as numerical goals Individual system diagrams by business unit
CSFs	Product and services rated by customer	Products and services rated by customer Functional performance Speed
Competitors' plans	Spotty to none	Both goals and plans
NCs	DoDs, some data-based	DoD, all data-based
Obstacles	Verbal gap statements	Strictly numerical gaps
Commitments	DoDs, some data-based	DoDs, all data-based
Milestones	None or few	Complete, both for necessary conditions and commitments
Timing	One full working day	2 full working days

Figure 15.5 Operational planning workshop – Two versions
To start, a good enough or light version should be used, to be refined at the next deep review.

Workshop agenda

The agenda for an operational planning workshop comprises six steps: Introduction, setting the operational goal, mapping the business system, designing the operational plan, setting the key events schedule and concluding the event.

---

1. **Introduction: Why we are here**
   - Our operational leadership methodology
   - Workshop outcomes: Operational goal, plan and key events schedule
2. **Operational goal**
   - Agreed-upon goal chart
3. **Business system**
   - Agree on business system
4. **Operational plan**
   - Develop operational plan
   - Final review of goal and plan
5. **Key events schedule**
   - Plan-Execute-Check cycle
   - Dates of quick and deep reviews
6. **Conclusion**
   - Call to action: Confirm obligations
   - Summing up

Figure 15.6 Operational planning workshop - Agenda
Six steps for preparing to execute.

Workshop step 1: Introduction

Unit managers must open and lead the operational planning workshops. For launching the use of PEC cycles, the message they give should be clear: "We are here today to design our first operational plan. This is not a seminar. This is a method that we need to become experts in, and it is how we want to manage our business operations moving forward." Leaders should be clear that this is not a "flavor of the month." Rather, it is a methodology that everyone will be expected to learn and use effectively.

For rebuilding a plan managers should emphasize the goal of the workshop: "To find out how our team can do better".

Workshop step 2: Set the operational goal

Launching PEC cycles

The outcome of this step is a goal chart, agreed to by the entire operational team.

This step depends largely on how thoroughly operational goals were defined prior to the workshop. There are typically two situations that occur:

If a goal chart already exists, review it for the right content and readiness for execution, and ensure the commitment of the unit owner and owners of sub-units. If a goal is defined, but not yet visible in a goal chart, design that goal chart in the workshop.

If operational goals are not yet available it may take as much as several hours to reach agreement. Present habits of goal setting (especially setting goals for efficiency, multiple goal setting and inflating goals) may need to be challenged and revised. It is critical to arrive at agreement on all items, applying the principles described in Chapter 4 (Right goals).

Rebuilding operational plans

In this case a short discussion and re-confirmation of the operational goal might be useful.

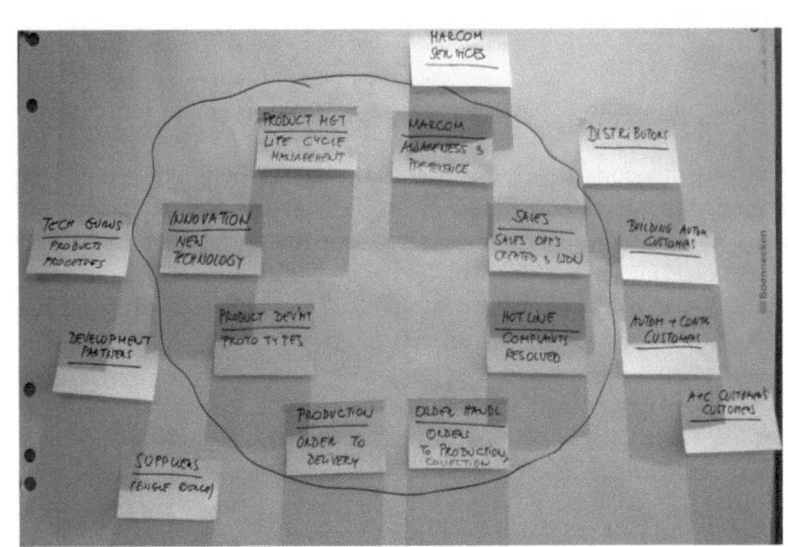

Figure 15.7 Mapping the business system (Draft, light version)
Business functions are named with their contribution, both internally and as external elements of the business ecosystem.

Workshop step 3: Map the business system

Launching PEC cycles

As basis for developing the operational plan, the operational team needs to agree on the internal and external elements of the business ecosystem. This agreement is best documented in a system diagram developed by the operational team.

Rebuilding operational plans

For rebuilding operational plans, an update of the existing business system chart could be of value.

Workshop step 4: Design the operational plan

In this step, starting from the critical success factors, develop the operational plan – in the full version all the way through to the milestones for necessary conditions and commitments. When the plan is finished, it is a good practice to let the owner of the plan (in the case of a top level plan, the CEO) walk the whole team through the plan verbally, answering clarifying questions and making final adjustments.

Chapter 15: Right operational leadership

Workshop step 5: The key events schedule

The heart of leading the PEC cycle is the schedule of quick and deep reviews, the key events schedule.

If operational plans are in use at several levels of the company, these reviews should be cascaded upwards: that is, start at the lowest level of the organizational business units and go upwards from there, level by level.

This way systemic obstacles can be identified and decisions can be made about where their resolution should be owned.

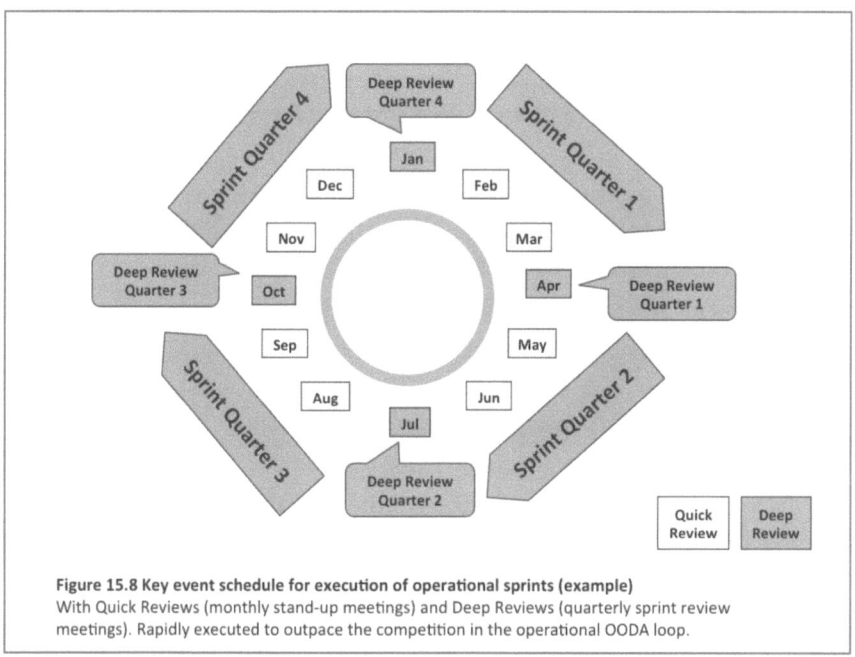

Figure 15.8 Key event schedule for execution of operational sprints (example)
With Quick Reviews (monthly stand-up meetings) and Deep Reviews (quarterly sprint review meetings). Rapidly executed to outpace the competition in the operational OODA loop.

The cadence of the key events schedule should be set with the goal of outpacing competitors.

Especially if the operational team is new to agile operational leadership, it is important to explain how critical a high cadence in the PEC cycle is and how the entire team must work together in execution.

Three rules for success of operational planning workshops

1. Management must lead the event

As the operational leader you own the quality of every single operational goal and plan in the business system - for your own business unit as well as for all of its lower level units. There is no way to delegate this - not to the controller, to other staff functions or to a computer system. They may help; but you own the process and the outcome.

Jim Arthur, Executive VP, WW sales executive for HP's computer business, had no doubt about his job to make sure that operational goals and plans in his organization were perfect. Before the start of every fiscal year, after every sales unit had done it's planning, he visited each of them and reviewed their operational goals and plans. With his sign-off he approved implementation. He fully owned the quality of these plans.

The operational planning workshop is the key event for the operational team to develop the right operational plans. If you do not lead this key event in person, you might as well forget the rest.

2. A workshop for the entire operational team

This event was very important for me, personally. It is now for the first time, that I see the value I add to the whole team, and how we all work together. Participant at a successful operational planning workshop.

The entire operational team must participate in the operational planning workshop. Every team member must have the opportunity to contribute to the design of each element of the operational plan.

There is a tendency to consider having operational plans developed by a small core team and then invite the other members of the operational team to review and comment. That won't work. The entire team needs to be there to ensure - in sometimes-intense discussion - that the obligations within their operational plan fit together with respect to cause and effect. In addition, it is a more efficient use of time to convene in the operational planning workshop than to draft a plan, incorporate comments and confirm all obligations separately.

Having the entire operational team actively participate is of special importance when rebuilding an operational plan after an operational sprint review. You must have everyone's experience and competence as sources for building a better plan for the next sprint.

3. Don't rush

The operational plan is the surfboard for riding the monster waves of opportunity. Quickly nailing and gluing one together won't get you to the top of any wave.

A well-thought-out operational plan will require hours of intensive work and several kilos of paper. William A. Woehr.

Designing an operational plan is top-level work for the *data-driven System 2*. This work requires intensive and tiring mental effort.

(Our data-driven) System 2 is the only one that can follow rules, compare objects on several attributes and make deliberate choices between options ... the defining feature of System 2 is that its operations are effortful[71]

---

[71] Kahneman, Daniel: Thinking, fast and slow. McMillan, 2011.

Leading key event No.2: Meetings

Every meeting you attend is an opportunity to emphasize the focus on operational goals and delivery of necessary conditions. There are just two items to present and discuss: "Before we start, let me give you an update on how we are doing with our goals and our necessary conditions".

Share the goal chart in every meeting

The job of operational leaders is to constantly keep every person in the business system – not just the operational team - aware of and focused on the operational goals.

> *John Young, CEO of HP from 1977–1992, focused HP as a whole on his personal goal. He had identified HP's low competence in TQM as a systemic obstacle. To resolve it he launched his "10X" project. The DoD of this project was reduction of the company's effort for warranty to one tenth of what is was at project start. Every division had to drive this project. John Young reviewed it at every occasion, asking, "How are you helping me to achieve my goal?" (The goal was achieved exactly.)*

As operational leaders, present and discuss progress to operational goals on your goal chart – always up to date – at every meeting (see example in Chapter 13, Right execution).

Share progress in necessary conditions

The second piece of information to share is progress in achieving necessary conditions. This demonstrates focus on the few initiatives that are vital to the future of the company, and that this process is not just talk, but a non-negotiable requirement of employment.

Most important is to share progress against necessary conditions for the entire plan as well as the individual NC's DoDs (Definition of Done) presented by its goal chart, or progress in delivery of obligations. (Both are discussed in Chapter 13, Right execution).

Leading key event No. 3: Quick Review

Following agile principles, while executing operational sprints conduct stand-up meetings. In these quick reviews, review progress on the path to achieving goals and in delivering necessary conditions. Goal charts and operational plans are already designed for efficient and effective quick reviews.

	Details
Date, location	Fixed well in advance – no surprise reviews
Plans reviewed	One at a time
Goal	Update on progress in goals and necessary conditions
Participants	Operational team of plan reviewed
Time	Time limited to 1 hour
	Agenda
What was achieved?	1. Accomplishments of goals 2. Delivery of necessary conditions. Special attention to NCs aimed at resolving constraints
What comes next?	3. Forecast and obstacles for goals 4. NCs: Milestones due in next period, obstacles
Adjusting accountability	5. Changes in organization, ownership
Other items are noted for discussion afterwards	

Figure 15.9 Quick review: Monthly sprint review meeting
The most effective and efficient meeting must be: limited to 1 hour, focused on the essentials of executing the operational plans.

Management must lead

The eye of the master fattens his cattle.[72]

A quick review must not just be a compilation of written reports. Instead, it is a critical reflection of how you progress to the operational goal and in the initiatives designed to reach it.

Management must lead this event in person. The moment leaders drop this responsibility the operational team's focus on execution will deteriorate.

---

[72] This proverb is known worldwide – we found it in Germany (where it is the title of a fairy tale), in the U.S. and in Japan

As scheduled

In the planning workshop, we set the schedule for quick reviews. This schedule is cast in concrete – the dates will not be changed for any reason.

One plan at a time

Nothing is a more boring waste of time for anyone than attending the quick review of a plan that she or he is not involved in. Strong quick reviews cover one plan at a time, and only owners of obligations in that plan attend.

Time-boxed

Following the practice of agile software development a quick review is limited to one hour.

Focused on just five elements

What was achieved?

1. How were goals accomplished? Data and comments discussed by the goal owner.
2. How did we deliver against necessary conditions and their milestones (intermediate DoDs)?

What comes next?

3. Forecast for our goals. Is there a foreseeable constraint? Yes? Plan a deep review to adjust the plan.
4. Necessary conditions. Milestones due in the next sprint (month). Has any new obstacle surfaced?

Adjustment in accountability for obligations required?

5. Who has changed jobs? Who has joined or left the operational team? Obligations may need to be reassigned.

Other items

Items not related to elements of the operational plan are identified and assigned to owners for discussion after - not during - the quick review.

Leading key event No.4: Deep review

Don't nobody bring no bad news

Some managers are tempted to be "good news" leaders. They only want to hear good news. This attitude unfortunately deprives them of the opportunity to learn how to improve their operational plans. Their people will turn to be "reporters of green"[73], only bringing good news. Pretty soon such managers lose contact with reality and thus the ability to steer their business to success.

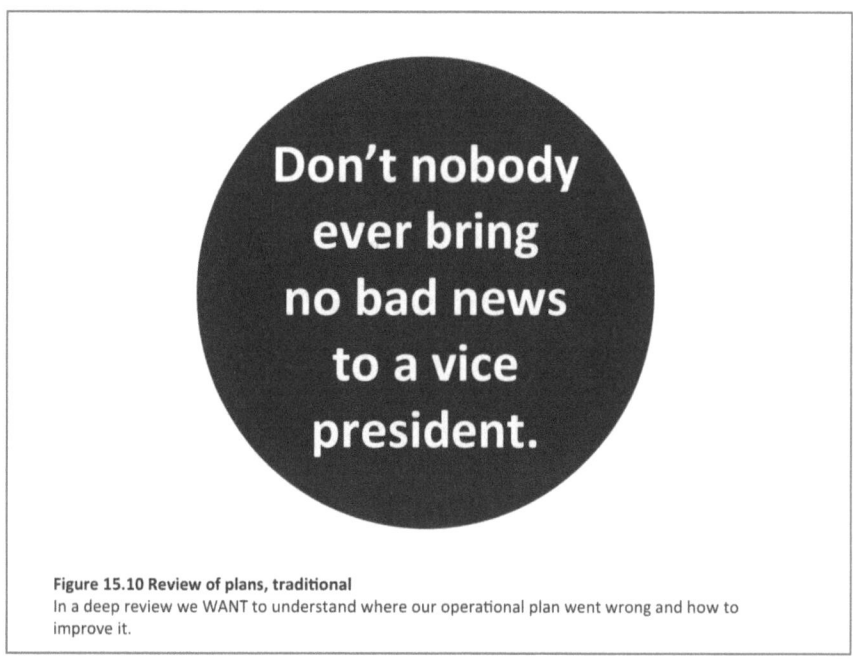

Figure 15.10 Review of plans, traditional
In a deep review we WANT to understand where our operational plan went wrong and how to improve it.

Contrary to this mistake the deep review is the event for checking plans and deciding whether they need to be improved, or as some managers say, if we are "in the right jungle." Have we identified the right critical success factors and necessary conditions? Will we outperform the market? Are we ahead of our competitors and trends in technology, supply chain, marketing, and sales?

---

[73] A free translation of the German term „Grünmelder", describing the job of people who report state of the business in traffic light schemes, and are expected to report „All green, boss"

Management must lead deep review of own plan

Operational leadership for each unit MUST lead these reviews. Particularly if the unit faces a constraint, leadership must actively participate in identifying it and planning its resolution. This means leading the active participation of all team members through questions and suggestions, not leading by monologue, with the rest of the participants remaining mute.

Management must attend deep review of all their units

Managers must attend deep reviews for units reporting to them as well. Remember: managers own the quality of the operational plans of all units reporting to them.

Agenda tuned to quadrant of operational excellence

The agenda of a deep review depends on the position in one of the four quadrants of the business unit being reviewed (see Chapter 14, Right check).

	Details		
Date, location	Fixed well in advance – no surprise reviews		
Plans reviewed	One at a time		
Goal	Update on progress against goals and necessary conditions		
Participants	Operational team of plan reviewed		
Time	Depending on position in quadrant: 1-2 days		
	Agenda		
Excellent operational leadership (1/2-1 day)	Lucky win (1 day)	Wrong plan (1-2 days)	Got it wrong (2 days)
• Refine plan • Assign deep review obligations	• Find constraint in obligations pipeline • Plan to resolve • Rebuild plan • Assign deep review obligations	• Find root cause constraint • Plan to resolve • Rebuild plan • Assign deep review obligations	• Find root cause constraint • Find constraint in obligations pipeline • Plan to resolve • Rebuild plan • Assign deep review obligations
	New or modified business units: Operational planning workshop		

Figure 15.11 Deep review: The operational sprint review meeting
Agenda tuned to the unit's position in the quadrants of operational performance.

As scheduled

The key events schedule determined that deep reviews are events of the highest priority. Their dates are firm, and they are not to be changed under any circumstances. If leaders let them slip they are indicating that these reviews are not that important. As a result, focus on and dedication to the operational effort will deteriorate.

Whole team event

The entire operational team works on the plan. That means, that the entire team must participate.

Don't rush

Again, no rush. As with operational planning, deeply reviewing a plan is hard work for the *data-driven System 2*.

There is no way to develop a valid CRT in just an hour - the more complex the cause/effect network, the longer it will take to find the root cause constraint.

Leading competence in PEC cycles

Competence in PEC (Plan-Execute-Check) cycles is a necessary condition for operational excellence. Leading that competence consists of assessing the present level and then planning for further development as part of the operational plan.

	Level	Methods	Use	Results
5	Can teach	Many new methods developed	Everywhere	Far ahead of competitors
4	Can lead	A few new methods developed	Many places	Clearly ahead of competitors
3	Can do	Full range of existing methods known	Several places	Ahead of competitors in some areas
2	Can talk	Some existing methods known	Few instances	Behind competitors
1	Cannot talk	Unknown	Nowhere	None

Figure 15.12 Levels of competence
Operational competence shows in results achieved through use of proven methods known and used widely.

Assessing competence

To assess operational competence Soin Singh recommends asking three questions:[74]

1) Do we know methods to address the challenges we face?
2) Beyond knowing such methods - do we actually use them?
3) We know methods and use them: do we achieve good results?

---

[74] Soin, Sarv Singh: Total quality essentials. Updated edition. McGraw Hill, New York. 1992

Take for example designing an operational plan. The method may be well understood, but it is only used in one of five units. The system in its entirety therefore is unable to achieve results and thus falls short of competitors.

In this case, score methods at 3, use at 2 and results at 2. To determine the overall score for this item, take the average (3+2+2)/3= 2.3.

Checklists competence in PEC cycles

On the following pages the key criteria for success for each step of the PEC cycle is listed, as described in detail in the previous chapters.

These tables can be used to assess the competence of the business, step by step. A best practice would be to do the assessment with the entire operational team, so that everyone agrees on strengths and opportunities for improvement.

These checklists deliver a sound assessment of competency in the steps of the PEC cycle. Areas of insufficient competence are candidates for initiatives in the operational plans.

1. Competence in setting the right goals		Score
Right content	* Single operational goal: Contribution margin. * Productivity as CSF or NC. * Matrix goals clear. * Goals set for breakthrough. * Goals not inflated. * Incentive goals separate from operational goals.	
Right for leading execution	* Goal charts of utmost simplicity. * Correct internediate goals. ** Milestones set. ** Hockeystick goals double-checked. ** Product rollovers included. ** Right seasonality. * Single accountable owners. ** No team goals. ** Matrix challenge resolved.	

Chapter 15: Right operational leadership

		Score
2. Competence in designing the right plans		
Principles	* Goals deployed top down. * Unit plans autonomous. * Systemic constraints addressed at higher level. * Matrix plans are sub-plans of hierarchy plans. * Cross functional plans in income generating units.	
Critical success factors	* Serve short term and longer range goals. * Phrased as states. * Social dimension considered (emotions, culture). * Entire business system checked. * Causal necessity for goals confirmed. * CSFs separate from NCs.	
Competitors' plans	* Key competitors selected. * Competitors' plans operationalized. ** Data, not anecdotes. ** Customer view of products and services known. ** Customer view of function performance known. ** Compettitors' speed in functions and PEC cycle known.	
Necessary conditions	* NCs are operationalized. ** Clear DoDs. ** Single accountable owners. ** Assigned at right level. ** Milestones defined. * All NCs identified. * Competitors' plans preempted/neutralized.	
Obstacles	* Obstacles are operationalized. ** Function identified. ** Phrased as function performance gaps. ** One obstacle per statement. * Entire business system checked. * Emotional obstacles considered.	
Commitments	* Commitments are operationalized. ** Phrased as DoDs. ** Single DoDs per statement. ** Single accountable owners. ** Due dates defined. ** Milestones defined. * Phrased to overcome obstacle. * Entire business system checked. * Causal connection to obstacle proven.	
Key events schedule	* Quick & deep reviews scheduled 12 months in advance.	
Obligations confirmed	* All obligations confirmed.	

Chapter 15: Right operational leadership

		Score
3. Competence in executing operational plans		
Focus on goals	* Operational team's goal progress and forecast clear. * Forecast with high accuracy.	
Managing obligations	* Obligations logged. * Weekly obligation sprints. * Operational team updated. * Obligations delivered complete, on time. * Obligations closed.	
Quick reviews	* Prepared: Comments on goals and necessary conditions. * Done on schedule. * Special attention on necessary conditions. * Time-boxed. * Other items covered later.	
Key events schedule	* Strictly adhered to.	

		Score
4. Competence in checking operational plans (Deep reviews)		
Agenda	* Led by unit and top managers. * No rush. Sufficient time. * Tuned to quadrant of performance.	
Finding root cause constraints	* Searching for causal clusters (4 column table). * Root cause constraint identified (CRT).	
Plan to resolve	* Constraint resolution plans designed. * Impact of injection tested (FRT).	

		Score
5. Competence in leading PEC cycles		
Leading Operational Planning Workshops	* Management leads. * Whole operational team participates. * Sufficient time. No rush. * Perfectly prepared: All required information available. * Clear operational goal defined, logged on goal chart. * Business system mapped. * Operational plan completed. * Key events schedule defined.	
Leading Meetings	* Goal chart shared - Achievements, forecasts. * Progress in NCs shared.	
Leading Quick reviews	* Management leads. * As scheduled. * One plan at a time. * Time-boxed and focused. * Accountability changes done. * "Other" items moved to "later".	
Leading Deep reviews	* Management leads. * As scheduled. * Whole operational team participates. * No rush.	

Summary of assessment and action plan

For a better overview, summarize your assessment using a radar graph as shown:

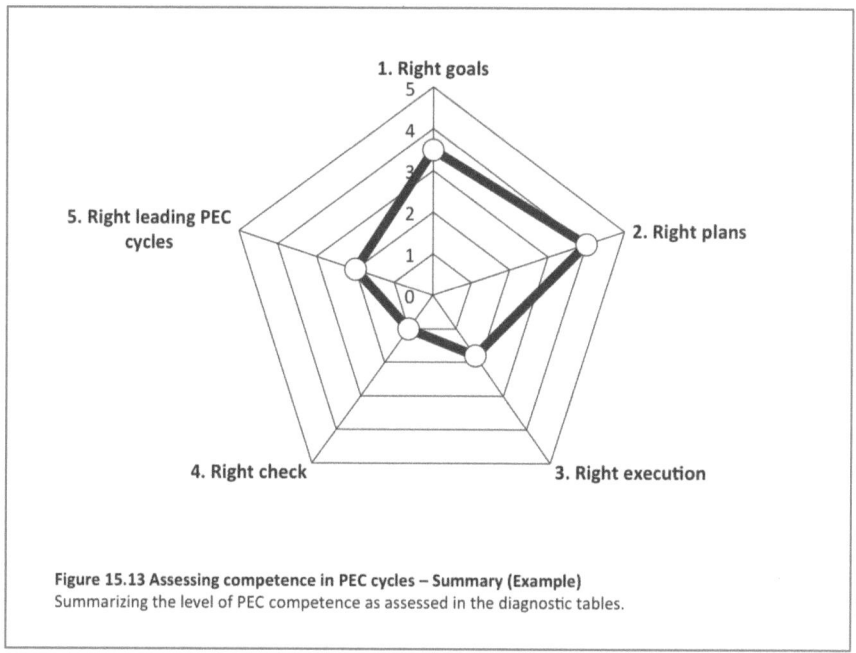

Figure 15.13 Assessing competence in PEC cycles – Summary (Example)
Summarizing the level of PEC competence as assessed in the diagnostic tables.

In that example there is need to focus on improving the effectiveness of operational leadership. Low competence in quick and deep reviews may be caused by lack of adherence to the key events schedule or lack of management presence at reviews.

To improve competence, add required initiatives as either critical success factor or necessary conditions to the operational plan, at the top management level.

Leading a culture of operational excellence

Beyond competence in PEC (Plan-Execute-Check) cycles, to reach and sustain operational excellence the business team needs a fundamental set of shared values, of "how we do things here." These values determine the culture of operational excellence.

The HP Way - leading example of culture of operational excellence

In 1957 HP was still a small company. Even so, Bill Hewlett and Dave Packard saw that it was necessary to define their company's culture - the values of how they wanted things to be done at HP.

Any organization, any group of people who have worked together for some time, develops a philiosphy, a set of values, a seris of traditions and customs ... deeply held beliefs that guide us in meeting our objectives, in working with one another and in dealing with customers, shareholders, and others.[75]

Today we recognize The HP Way[76] as a leading example of a culture of operational excellence.

Five values determine the culture of operational excellence

Since 1957 many executives from other companies have followed HP's example and stated the values they expect their people to embody. Five values consistently appear in these statements: breakthrough goals, teamwork, agility, management's contribution and positive emotions.

(To describe a culture of low operational excellence simply turn each statement into its opposite. "Here, everyone takes it easy, we focus on what's in it for ourselves, we move slowly, our managers block progress and we hate to work here")

Let's discuss these five values of operational excellence in detail.

---

[75] Dave Packard, quoted in Malone, Michael S.: Bill and Dave, how Hewlett and Packard built the world's greatest company. Portfolio/Penguin Group, New York. 2007.

[76] http://www.hpalumni.org/hp_way.htm

Chapter 15: Right operational leadership

We have trust and respect for individuals.
We approach each situation with the belief that people want to do a good job and will do so, given the proper tools and support. We attract highly capable, diverse, innovative people and recognize their efforts and contributions to the company. HP people contribute enthusiastically and share in the success that they make possible.

We focus on a high level of achievement and contribution.
Our customers expect HP products and services to be of the highest quality and to provide lasting value. To achieve this, all HP people, especially managers, must be leaders who generate enthusiasm and respond with extra effort to meet customer needs. Techniques and management practices which are effective today may be outdated in the future. For us to remain at the forefront in all our activities, people should always be looking for new and better ways to do their work.

We conduct our business with uncompromising integrity.
We expect HP people to be open and honest in their dealings to earn the trust and loyalty of others. People at every level are expected to adhere to the highest standards of business ethics and must understand that anything less is unacceptable. As a practical matter, ethical conduct cannot be assured by written HP policies and codes; it must be an integral part of the organization, a deeply ingrained tradition that is passed from one generation of employees to another.

We achieve our common objectives through teamwork.
We recognize that it is only through effective cooperation within and among organizations that we can achieve our goals. Our commitment is to work as a worldwide team to fulfill the expectations of our customers, shareholders and others who depend upon us. The benefits and obligations of doing business are shared among all HP people.

We encourage flexibility and innovation.
We create an inclusive work environment which supports the diversity of our people and stimulates innovation. We strive for overall objectives which are clearly stated and agreed upon, and allow people flexibility in working toward goals in ways that they help determine are best for the organization. HP people should personally accept responsibility and be encouraged to upgrade their skills and capabilities through ongoing training and development. This is especially important in a technical business where the rate of progress is rapid and where people are expected to adapt to change.

Figure 15.14 The HP Way – Leading example of the culture of operational excellence

Breakthrough goals culture

Breakthrough goals culture reveals constraints

Only by setting breakthrough goals will our business system's constraints be revealed. They are the catalyst to change course on the wave, not to just adjust the position of the surfboard.

We set breakthrough goals

We set breakthrough goals for ourselves and our operational teams, not goals that keep the business system in its comfort zone.

High level of achievement is the norm

We consider 100% achievement of our goals to be acceptable and more than 100% to be good performance. Achieving 99% is not good enough. Once we have set goals we focus on achieving them and not letting go, like a dog with its bone. We value stick-to-it-iveness and consistency of purpose.

Leading a breakthrough goals culture

We challenge comfort goals

As operational leaders we challenge comfort goals and set and lead to breakthrough goals.

> *For next year, our CEO has given us a comfort goal, one we will achieve easily. I feel insulted, because this means that he does not believe that we can resolve our constraints.*[77]

We focus our people on goals

We seek every opportunity to remind our people (and ourselves) of our operational goals, and share progress and the outlook in forecasts.

We lead by example

Everyone knows that we will always achieve our operational goals. We are pure examples of consistency of purpose.

---

[77] Manuel F. Diaz, head of Worldwide Sales for Hewlett-Packard's (HP) Computer Systems Organization (now retired) in a speech to HPs worldwide sales management.

Team culture

Team culture lets teams achieve more than the sum of individuals

Our effectiveness and efficiency to a large degree depends on how we serve each other. Thus as teams we strive to produce results that are more than the sum of what each of us could achieve alone: we contribute value to each other, speak up when we see opportunity for improvement and keep our promises, always.

We contribute value to each other

> *In the polar region trappers have a life-saving habit. Before leaving a shelter and moving on to the next they arrange wood, paper and matches in the oven, ready for use and covered to keep it dry. So when the next one arrives, perhaps close to freezing to death he or she can count on it only being a matter of seconds to have a fire burning. They do this without any idea who the next one will be. This is what I call caring for other people.*[78] *Christiane Ritter*

Externally, we offer products and services to our customers that will help them to achieve their own goals, by resolving their constraints.

Within our company we seek to contribute value to everyone we serve. Our motto is "What is in it for you?" rather than "What is in it for me?"

For example, we design products to maximize ease of use by others with respect to manufacturability, ease of delivery, ease of installation, and ease of use by the end user.

No fear of speaking up

We value people who voice their views constructively, especially when they are in striking contradiction to what others think and say. We do not value people if they don't speak up when they have a different view.

Promise made, promise kept

We know that our ability to achieve our goals depends on a culture of high reliability. Many of the functions and people are positioned elsewhere in the business ecosystem and therefore do not report to us. Yet we depend on the reliability of customers, suppliers and advisors, just to name a few.

---

[78] Personal narration by Christiane Ritter, author of 'A woman in the Polar night', never out of print since it was first published in 1938.

Low reliability forces the "next in flow" to waste time and capacity, in both preventing and recovering from the broken promises of others.

We value reliability. We keep our promises, individually and as teams. Whatever we promise we deliver, on time and complete, always. Why? Because that is the way we do it here.

Leading team culture

Ensure achievement of necessary conditions

As operational leaders we ensure the success of any cross functional project or process. Most importantly, we help achieve or lead to our NCs, which are often cross-function projects.

Zero tolerance for low reliability

We lead our people to understand why it is important to deliver obligations as committed. We show zero tolerance for broken promises. Unreliable people must change - or leave.

Ensure sharing of goals and plans

We insist that goals, plans and progress in both are shared. All team members must understand their contribution to operational excellence and the results those contributions achieve.

Leading example of team culture

We perceive ourselves as members of our operational teams, not as rulers of slaves. As such, we are examples of contributing value to others. We ensure that whatever we do adds value to the efforts of our operational team. We exhibit rock-solid reliability, always on time and delivering what we promised.

Agile culture

Business agility is the ability of a business system to rapidly respond to change[79] by adapting its initial stable configuration.

In a business context, agility is the ability of an organization to rapidly adapt to market and environmental changes in productive and cost-effective ways. The agile enterprise is an extension of this concept, referring to an organization that utilizes key principles of complex adaptive systems and complexity science to achieve success.

Teams with agile culture never are complacent

The waves we surf along with our competitors move and change all the time. Our ability to observe and adapt both our position and how we move on the wave determines our success. The shorter our reaction time to newly discovered opportunities to improve our plans, the better we will surf our wave.

We spin our PEC cycles fast

We lead our business system's agility by spinning our PEC (Plan-Execute-Check) cycles.

With eyes and ears wide open we actively seek to quickly recognize obstacles and constraints, decide how to resolve them, and execute the related projects.

Leading agile culture

The heartbeat of an agile culture is the speed at which we spin our PEC (Plan-Execute-Check) cycles. We lead that with the frequency of our quick and deep reviews.

To lead agility, we organize in units of high autonomy for operational planning, execution and adjustment of plans. We decentralize everything but crucial infrastructure[80] and have decisions made at the lowest possible level.

When we leave key events of operational leadership we have induced forward-looking, agile creativity in participants.

---

[79] https://en.wikipedia.org/wiki/Business_agility

[80] House, Charles H. and Price, Raymond L.: The HP Phenomenen. Stanford University Press. 2009

Managers are not the constraint

There's bad news and good news. The bad news first: without being aware of it, we managers often constrain the business system's performance. The good news: we can fix this.

The most frequent ways in which we may constrain the performance of the business system is by not being content experts, not spending enough time on operational leadership and by working practices that slow down or hinder communications and decision-making.

Managers are content experts

To understand the business system's constraints we must acquire a deep understanding of that system, become content experts.

It is also essential that the manager have a thorough knowledge and understanding of the work of his or her group. ... I don't see how managers can even understand what standards to observe, what performance to require, and how to measure results unless they understand in some detail the specific nature of the work they are trying to supervise.[81]

---

[81] Dave Packard, The HP Way. How Bill Hewlett and I built our company. Harper Business.1995

Managers spend sufficient time on operational leadership

As managers we should be spending the majority of our time on operational leadership, as described in the Itoh model[82] (see the illustration above).

Unfortunately, real life is different. The higher we progress in management the less time we have to do what we want to do.

> *In a good week, I can decide what I want to do for 25% of my time. Marcel Ospel, former Chairman UBS Switzerland, interview on Swiss television.*

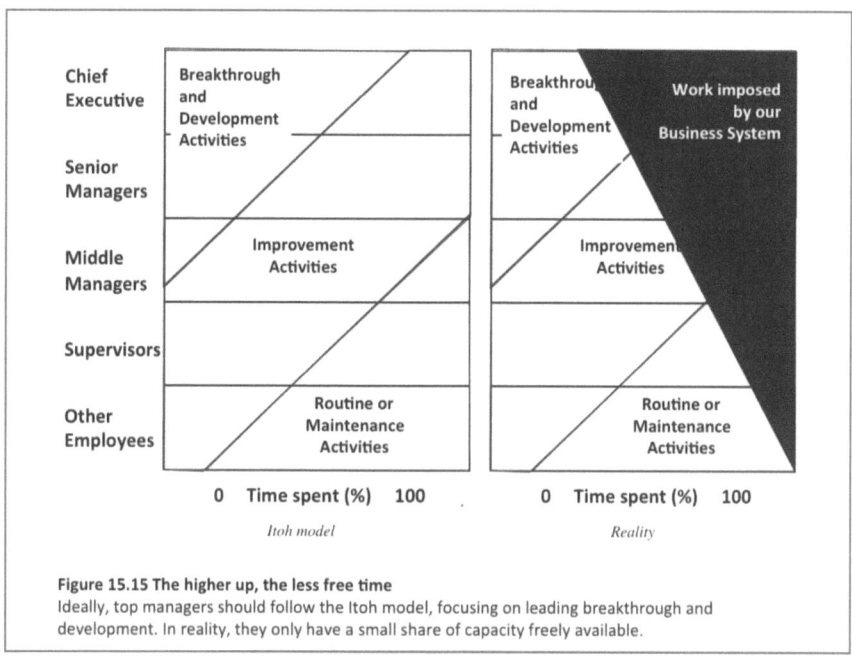

Figure 15.15 The higher up, the less free time
Ideally, top managers should follow the Itoh model, focusing on leading breakthrough and development. In reality, they only have a small share of capacity freely available.

At any time, any part of our business system may interrupt what we planned to do and ask us for help. Customers, suppliers or partners may require instant access at any time. Our internal functions may ask us to help close a big deal, resolve a serious service issue, decide on a personnel matter or approve a key decision.

This fact of life constrains our capacity for operational leadership. How to cope?

---

[82] Discussed in Soin, Sarv Singh: Winning with operational excellence. 2013. p.223-224

Delegating operational leadership is not an option

Some managers may view operational leadership as something for lower level management that doesn't require their involvement. They could not be more wrong. Delegating operational leadership? Don't even think about it. Let's hope that you never author a memo like the one below. Or even think that way.

Email from CEO, to all managers:

It has been brought to my attention that many of you feel I should worry more about how you execute the strategy that we defined last September.

Let me set this straight: As CEO, my job is to define the strategy. As managers of this company your job is to execute. My job therefore is not to check whether you execute.

CEO, S.R.N (fired after having missed operational goals eight quarters in a row)

Operational excellence is an unstable state - like surfing big waves. As with surfing, to lead or keep a business system at top level requires constant attention and effort. The moment operational leadership is delegated, focus on the operational goals fades away, delivery of operational obligations slips, resolution of constraints fails or is not even tackled, plans are not checked and adjusted. As a result, the business fails to achieve its operational goals and falls off the wave.

Solution: Exploit the constraint of management capacity

Eliyahu Goldratt described a five-step approach to addressing a constraint.[83] Step 1 is *Identify the constraint*. Step 2 is *Exploit the constraint*, that is, maximize the utilization and productivity of the constrained function.

Exploiting our time constraint as operational leaders means rigorously simplifying all work of operational leadership to a minimum. The practices discussed in this book make that possible:

1. Reduce the number of operational goals to just one. Any additional goal requires more of your capacity. Only use simple one-goal charts. The more simple goal charts are the less time is spent interpreting them.
2. Reduce the number of operational plans to one. Only use one-page constraint-focused plans, showcases of logical clarity.

---

[83] http://www.tocinstitute.org/five-focusing-steps.html

3. Ensure the top quality of operational plans. Any element that does not resolve obstacles or constraints and any rework caused by sloppy planning waste your capacity and that of your operational team.
4. Reduce the effort of leading execution to the vital few operational projects - necessary conditions. Only care about progress in these.
5. Resist the temptation to tackle new ideas intuitively. Refuse to take on any action or project not contained in the plan. Only add new initiatives to the operational plan if they improve its effectiveness or efficiency.
6. Reduce the number of meetings. Just do quick and deep reviews. Refuse to add other meetings to your key events schedule.
7. Keep quick reviews short: stand-up meetings, a hard stop after one hour.
8. Focus deep reviews on their purpose: to improve the effectiveness of the operational plans. Only that.

Managers communicate and decide fast

So how was Wayne Gretzky able to get a hockey shot off so quickly? A Canadian neurologist determined that Gretzky has the quickest reflexes ever measured by this specific neurologist. Gretzky's muscle movement controlled by long loops of brain cells within the motor cortex of the brain occurs exceptionally quickly. Thus, it is due to Gretzky's rapid brain cells that he was able to excel as he did in hockey.[84]

In our business system the speed at which its nervous system transmits signals determines its effectiveness. Consider the stream of messages the business system expects us to handle on a given day - phone calls, email, SMS, each requiring a decision. By not replying or deciding slowly we constrain communications and decision-making. As result, we limit the speed at which the business system performs its OODA loops.

To accelerate the speed of communications and decision-making, reduce the number of decisions required from you. Two of Dave Packard's principles of management show how to do that:

1) Let decisions be made at the lowest possible level. This principle eliminates waste of time by decisions going up and down hierarchical layers.

2) Decentralize. Avoid or central functions to the largest possible degree.

Instead of creating better focus and coordinating the business (across several units), centralized management resulted in decision cycle times ballooning.[85]

---

[84] http://serendip.brynmawr.edu/bb/neuro/neuro05/web1/avenditta.html

[85] Packard, David: The HP Way, How Bill Hewlett and I built our company. Harper Business.1995

Positive emotions culture

Open any book about business management and go to its index. Search for the word emotions. In most books you will not find a reference. How come? Are business companies just rational constructs, cold minded and fact driven? Are emotions just stupid behavior of people with low self-control?

Emotions? – Here at work? You must be joking. Here we work. Emotions we have at home. S.R.N.[86]

Wrong. Emotions play a major role in the performance of business systems. Positive emotions support performance, negative emotions constrain it.

Positive emotions support the business system's performance

- Strong positive emotion correlates with better financial results for an organization, as measured by five-year total shareholder return.
- Positive emotions encourage people to discover novel lines of thought or action.
- People are more likely to help others when feeling positive emotions.
- Positive emotions speed recovery from negative emotions, so they also fuel resilient coping.

Negative emotions constrain the business system's performance

Right now, there is an enormous gap between employees' current and ideal work experience. People know what they want and need to feel intensely positive about their work, but unfortunately many are not getting it. On average, more than half of people's current emotion at work is negative and a third is intensely negative.[87] *Without strong positive ties to work or the work experience, employees have little incentive to go the distance or deliver consistently top performance.*

Of those who are intensely negative about their current experience, 28 per cent are actively looking for a new job or are poised to leave when a new opportunity arises. (Among those who currently feel strongly positive, just six per cent are looking for a new job or are poised to leave). But nevertheless, a quarter of the intensely negative employees plan to remain with their current employer, just staying in "inner emigration".

---

[86] From Branka Zei-Pollermann

[87] Towers Perrin report "Working Today: Exploring Employee's Emotional Connection To Their Jobs", 2003

Assignments match skills

Job assignements, and especially operational obligations are set up to match the skills of our people, so they can experience growth and learning. In other words, "We are responsible for them to work in flow."[88]

Contribution is recognized

Sadly, about four out of every five employee contributions go unrecognized, according to at least one study. These management errors of omission are costly missed opportunities to pump up engagement levels.[89]

Recognizing a job well done? No way. If I do that people become arrogant and demand more money. Vice president of a bank, S.R.N.

This is really a no-brainer: Just do it. Say thank you for a job well done.

Zero tolerance for emotional abuse

Under no circumstances is there room for the emotional abuse that sometimes happens when some (emotionally incompetent) people play abusive games at the expense of others. Such persons have no place on the team.

Leading a positive emotions culture

Everyone understands our goals and plans

To lead a culture of positive emotions, make sure that everyone understands the purpose of the organization, and can fully apply their skills to the challenges at work.

Operational plans help with that: they show every member of the operational team the value of her or his contribution and they give other employees confidence that their managers are doing their best to lead the company to success.

Managers are leading examples of positive emotions

Like the great team captains in sports, managers are leading examples of positive emotions. They radiate confidence even in the most distressing situations.

---

[88] Mihaly Csikszentmihalyi: Good business. Leadership, flow and the making of meaning. Penguin Books. New York. 2004

[89] Branham, Leigh: The 7 hidden reasons employees leave. American Management Association, 2012

Assessing culture of operational excellence

Below we offer a checklist for assessing a culture of operational excellence. (Scoring as described before).

Culture of operational excellence		
Breakthrough goals culture Values	* Goals are breakthrough - not comfort. * High level of achievement is the norm. * Consistency of purpose.	
Leading	* Comfort goals are challenged. * Goals always in mind. * Managers are leading examples of breakthrough goals culture.	
Team culture Values	* Value contributed to others. * No fear to speak up. * Promise made, promise kept.	
Leading	* Success of NCs/cross functional projects ensured. * Zero tolerance for lack of reliability. * Goals and plans shared. * Managers are leading examples of team culture.	
Agile culture Values	* Fast PEC cycles. * Obstacles are foreseen. * Constraints quickly recognized. * Constraints quickly resolved.	
Leading	* Teams never complacent. * Organized for high autonomy of units/decentralization. * Managers are leading examples of agile culture.	
Managers not the constraint	* Managers are content experts. * Sufficient time for operational leadership. * Operational leadership is not delegated. * Manager's time constraint is resolved. * Managers communicate and decide quickly. * Decisions at lowest possible level. * Minimal centralization.	
Positive emotions culture - Values	* Assignments match skills. * Contribution is recognized. * Zero tolerance for emotional abuse.	
Leading	* Everyone understands the goals and plans. * Managers leading examples of positive emotions culture.	

Chapter 15: Right operational leadership

Summary of assessment and development plan

Let's now summarize our assessment to visualize the level of culture as it relates to achieving operational excellence.

Again, areas requiring improvement should be added to operational plans.

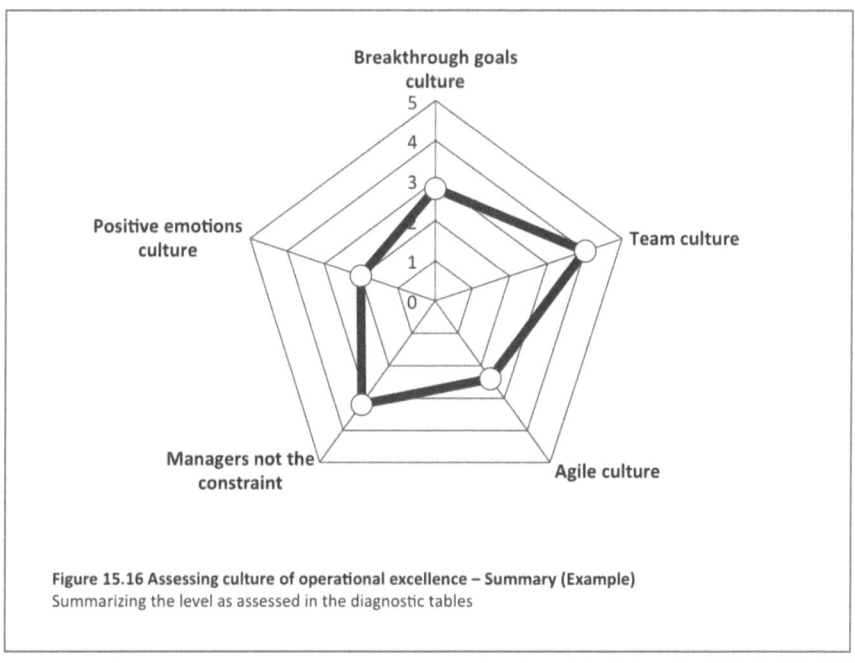

Figure 15.16 Assessing culture of operational excellence – Summary (Example)
Summarizing the level as assessed in the diagnostic tables

Chapter 16: Now, it's your turn

Chapter 16: Now, it's your turn

Thank you for staying with me through this book. I hope you feel that I kept my promise: to show operational leadership as a management discipline in its own right and the most fascinating and rewarding challenge in business management. This task is where we can do much more than think and talk intelligently. We can test our ability to bring our ideas into reality.

As operational leaders we have accepted responsibility of caring for a wonderful creature, gifted to achieve top-league performance in surfing the waves of opportunity.

It is our job as operational leaders to steer this great being on the giant waves we surf - to build an ideal surfboard (our operational plan) and then guide it to follow an ideal line on our wave.

To do so, we focus on the vital few things: critical success factors and their necessary conditions, in planning as well as in execution.

This book is meant as a guide for surfing at world-class level. Regardless of the level at which you surf the big waves of opportunity right now – I hope you find the knowledge contained in this book to be useful for becoming or coaching others to become master surfers.

All kinds of businesses require operational leadership

What we discussed in this book applies to any kind of business enterprise, in any industry and in any of their business units, of any size – from small start-up to global businesses.

If for example you lead a sales organization you lead the sales system, and lead it to spin its PEC cycle. If you lead a sales channel, you lead that channel's business system. If you lead a company's key account sales you lead an operational sales plan for each account (each will require different critical success factors).

If you lead a service organization you might need an operational plan at the top level and one for each service product lines.

Whichever it is, it does not matter: you always require operational leadership to lead your business to perform at operational excellence.

How to start

The time to start is now.

Diagnose the competence of your business in PEC (Plan-Execute-Check) cycles and in the culture of operational excellence – best with the involvement of your entire operational team. (Chapter 15, Right leadership).

Lead by example. Start with one single goal and operational plan: for your business or unit, at the top. Create your own goal chart and arrange an operational planning workshop for your business. Then, lead quick and deep reviews for at least 6 months, driven by you key events schedule.

When your operational team is comfortable with the PEC cycle, go one level lower. Assign operational goals to next level units and lead operational planning workshops with the unit managers. Then, help them to get going with their PEC cycles.

Enjoy

Surfing big waves is – as we said in our preface – high-performance sports.

It's a tough challenge and hard work. For you as a professional, however, each successfully completed PEC cycle is another successful surf on a monster wave.

You are stepping into liquid. You are stepping off solid ground into an element that is always changing and moving and it's surrounding you. And it feels good.[90]

Don't forget to enjoy it along the way– and then, go for the next one.

As I said at the beginning: you will become addicted to this sport!

Happy surfing!

Dieter Legat

---

[90] http://www.stepintoliquid.com/the-trailer/

Chapter 17: The DELTA T Cockpit[91]

Assume your operational plan comprises three critical success factors with two necessary conditions each. Further assume that to achieve each NC requires two commitments and you plan to track NCs monthly and commitments quarterly. In total these are 3+6+12+72+48=141 obligations assigned to several owners in just one plan.

Now, start execution of the operational plan.

- Obligation owners need to add their comments, visible to all members of the operational team.
- You need to compile the status by obligation for quick reviews and
- Assess if and how to change the plan's obligations quarterly, in deep reviews. Such changes are additional obligations.
- If owners change you need to re-assign obligations.

The sheer volume of obligations and data related to them may easily defy your best intention to perform operational leadership. (Assume that you want to establish operational plans for the relatively simple organization we used as example in Chapter 6 (Right operational plan), you would arrive at 141x9=1269 obligations needing to be managed).

Recognizing this challenge we designed the DELTA T Cockpit as management tool to take care of that complexity. We encourage readers to consider using this software solution as the backbone of their operational excellence implementation. It embodies the FIVE RIGHT methodology in an easy-to-use-and-understand interface that will guide the process, track and monitor results and accelerate the learning curve.

A brief description is included here.

More information at http://www.book-agile-operational-leadership.com.

---

[91] Why DELTA T? In Chapter 4 (Right goals) we discussed the necessity to set one single clear operational goal, income or contribution margin. Theory of constraints uses the term 'throughput' for this dimension of the goal, with T as acronym. The purpose of operational leadership is to increase T – so, we called the software DELTA T COCKPIT.

Chapter 17: The DELTA T Cockpit

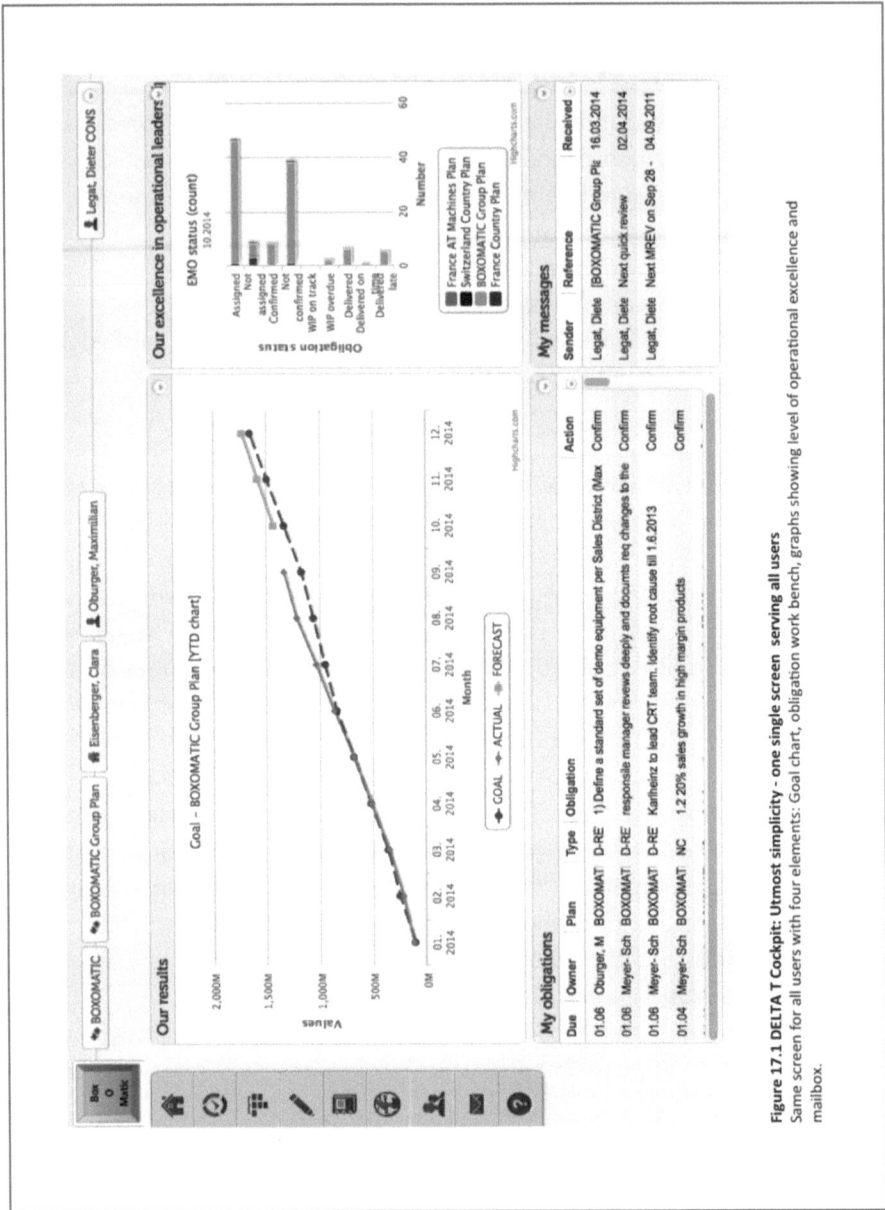

Figure 17.1 DELTA T Cockpit: Utmost simplicity - one single screen serving all users
Same screen for all users with four elements: Goal chart, obligation work bench, graphs showing level of operational excellence and mailbox.

184

The tool to support and simplify operational leadership

In design we put "utmost simplicity" as Number One priority. This resulted in one single layout of the user screen, no matter which role (obligation owner, unit manager, company manager) a user may have.

Just four elements on the single user screen

The common user screen contains four elements: the goal chart, an obligation workbench, a message box and a graphical view of the level of operational excellence.

Simple goal charts

Goal charts support the principle of "one single operational goal". They are prominently displayed, showing progress to the "to-date" goal and forecast. Other views (monthly, quarterly, annually, multiple periods) can be selected.

Simple operational planning

Logged "on the fly" in operational planning workshops, operational plans are displayed as one-page constraint focused plans in several views. All members of the operational team see their plan.

Simple review of all operational plans

Users can design a 'book of plans' containing all their operational plans.

Simple tracking of execution

Permanent focus on the goal

Goal charts are prominently displayed and visible to all members of operational teams.

Logging comments for goals, forecasts and obligations

Owners of goals can easily log comments on results and forecasts for information for their operational team and in preparation for quick and deep reviews. Owners of obligations can log comments on their progress.

Compiling information for quick reviews

Information for quick reviews can be compiled at any time, with a click on one single button: progress in goals, necessary conditions, commitments and milestones.

Chapter 17: The DELTA T Cockpit

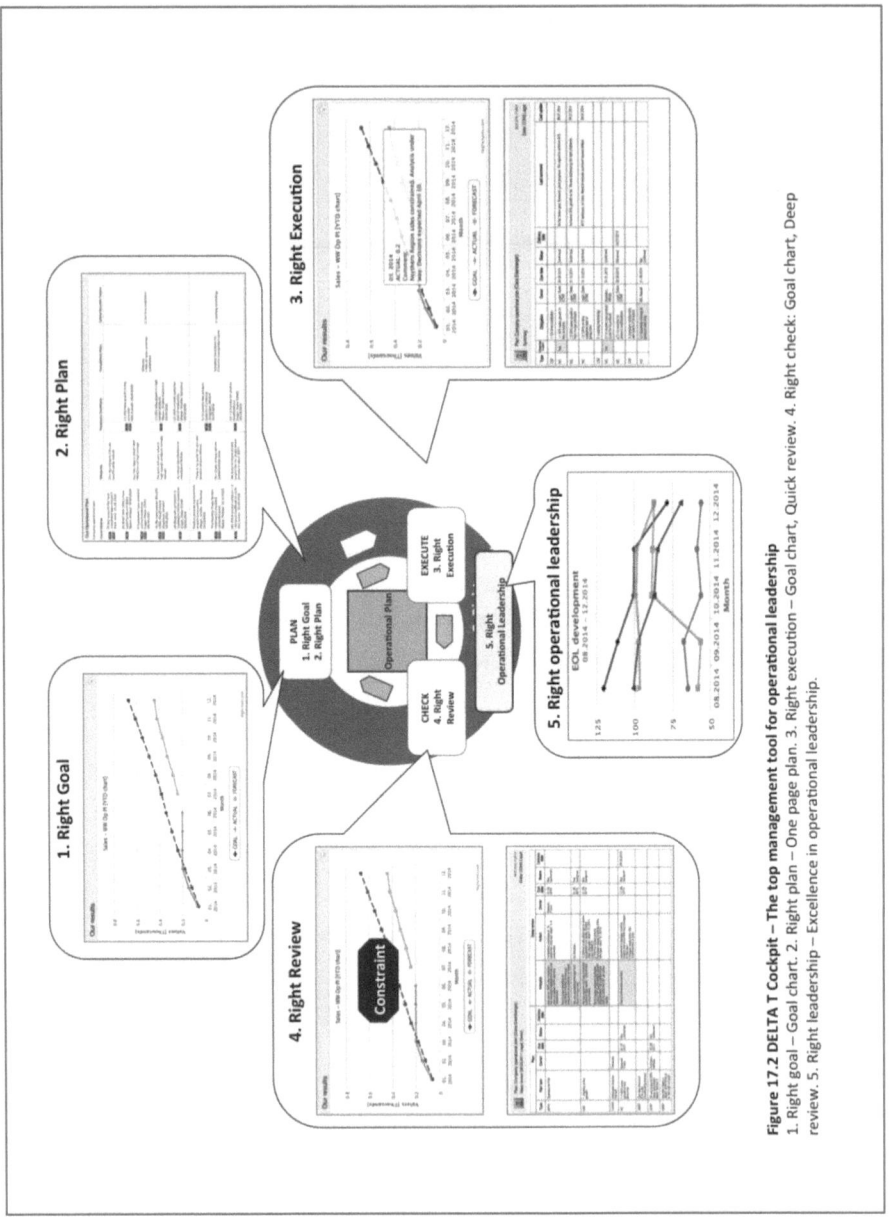

Figure 17.2 DELTA T Cockpit – The top management tool for operational leadership
1. Right goal – Goal chart. 2. Right plan – One page plan. 3. Right execution – Goal chart, Quick review. 4. Right check: Goal chart, Deep review. 5. Right leadership – Excellence in operational leadership.

Simple deep reviews

Users log their deep reviews "On the fly" in deep review meetings. Decisions to adjust the operational plan are logged, assigned and tracked through to delivery.

Simple tracking of excellence in operational leadership

As a special feature, the DELTA T Cockpit computes the EOL (excellence in operational leadership) indicator from both the level of achievement of goals and the performance in the obligations pipeline. Drill down through levels of the organization is available.

Scalable, flexible, worldwide access

The DELTA T Cockpit is designed for ease of use by operational leaders and their teams by these features:

Scalable

The DELTA T Cockpit is fully scalable to serve companies from small start-ups (one single operational plan) to large worldwide corporations. These may be organized in multiple hierarchies and matrix units (for example to lead product lines across geographical units), with an unlimited number of operational plans.

Flexible

Most companies have the need to frequently regroup their operational units – and thus, their operational plans. The DELTA T Cockpit is designed to cope with these changes.

Worldwide access

The tool is web based and accessible from anywhere in the world.

Thank you for teaching me

I am a very lucky person. Throughout my life I found people who taught me, opened my eyes for wider, bigger views. I owe to all the people who thus taught me. THANK YOU to all of my dear friends who helped me to learn what I offer in this book and in my consulting work about operational leadership. THANK YOU, to ..

Johannes E. Klinkmueller, my boss, coach and dear friend at Honeywell, who taught me about reliability more than anyone else in my life.

David Ellis-Jones and Don Halstead. Two marvelous management trainers, who introduced me to the realities of MbO, designing operational plans, and to problem analysis and resolution.

Franz Nawratil, who got me hired into HP and in this way, opened the door to HP. In many ways he was for me a leading example of HPs high performance culture.

Mario Fontana, my boss at HP Switzerland, who introduced me to many practices of operational excellence, and taught me the importance of key events schedules for operational excellence.

Bill Russell, my boss at HP Europe before he was promoted to worldwide responsibilities. What a great showcase of operational leadership he was.

Karen Slatford, my boss at HP after Bill Russell. Not only was she a master of operational leadership, she also was fully aware of the importance of the emotional and cultural dimensions of this task.

Hans-Peter Liebmann, who invited me to teach operational sales leadership at the University of Graz (my home town) and coached me in systems thinking for business, recommending the works of Maturana and Varela, Luhmann, von Foerster and other giants in system thinking.

The executives who allowed me to work for them to launch and use the PEC approach, as we call it now (in alphabetical sequence) - of Agie-Charmilles (Hakan Pfeiffer), BOBST Group (Jean-Pascal Bobst, Gabriel Migy and Nigel Tracey), DELL Computers (Alain Bandle and his team), Fujitsu-Siemens CEE (Tony Rozwadowski and his team), Haas Automation Europe (Jens Thing and his team), HP Telecom Business Unit (Sebastiano Tevarotto and his team), HP Russia (Owen Kemp and his team), as well as managers of OESSUR, SWISSQUOTE and other companies who gave invaluable feedback and recommendations for the methods presented in this book.

Abbreviations

BVI:	Brainstorm – vote - implement
CRT:	Current reality tree
CSF:	Critical success factors
DoD:	Definition of done
EOL:	Excellence in operational leadership
FRT:	Future reality tree
OODA:	Observe-orient-decide-act
PDC:	Plan-Do-Check
PDCA:	Plan-Do-Check-Act
PEC:	Plan-Execute-Check
PRT:	Prerequisite tree
S.R.N.	Shall remain nameless
TOC:	Theory of constraints
TQM:	Total quality management
WYSIATI:	What you see is all there is

Books

Here is a list of the books we referred to, extended by a few other books, which we used as cornerstones of the Five Right method:

About operational leadership

Drucker, Peter: The practice of management. (Harper Collins, New York. First published 1954)

The book in which MbO was presented the first time. In its time a break through to new thinking: away from command-and-control management to company wide goal setting, and some first ideas on participative management.

Soin, Sarv Singh: Total quality essentials. (Updated edition. McGraw Hill, New York. 1992)

Sarv Singh Soin was a key leader of HPs development of their quality culture, which today we would better call a culture of operational excellence. Its key contribution is that it goes far beyond quality methods. It describes operational leadership as a key process, which must be performed as impeccably as all other processes. A „how to" book for operational leaders.

Soin, Sarv Singh: Winning with operational excellence. (Sarv Singh Soin. 2013)

This is not a book about manufacturing theories – it's written by a practitioner for practitioners. An excellent quick and practical reference of leading practices.

Mintzberg, Henry: The rise and fall of strategic planning. (Simon and Schuster. 1994)

John Boyd: Presentations on OODA loop

John Boyd did not write books – he taught by giving many lectures and presentations. Here you find Boyd's major presentations in PDF format
This other presentation challenges command and control leadership.

Mihaly Csikszentmihalyi: Good business. Leadership, flow and the making of meaning.

(Penguin Books. New York. 2004). A sequel to his well-known book Flow; it extends his principles into the domain of leading businesses.

About systems

System theory has been a subject under constant development triggered by Ludwig von Bertallanffy in the early 1930ies.

Maturana, Humberto R. and Varela, Francisco J.: The tree of knowledge.

(Shambala. Boston & London, 1987)

Maturana and Varela, two biologists from Chile, in this book presented their concept of autopoietic (self-organizing and self-creating systems) for participants in courses they gave. Its fun to read and stretches the mind

Von Bertallanffy, Ludwig: General system theory. Foundations, development, applications. (George Braziller Inc. New York. 1969).

This is a newer edition of Bertallanffy ground-breaking thoughts.

About theory of constraints

For a start we found three books helpful – many more resources on TOC (books and videos) can be found at Goldratt Group

Goldratt, Eliyahu: The goal

This classic business novel (more than 1 million sold) lays out the principle of constraint thinking in a story of a manager solving his problems by TOC approach.

Goldratt, Eliyahu: What is this thing called TOC?

In this book Goldratt explains the principles of (and hurdles to) constraint-focused management.

Dettmer, H. William: The logical thinking process

(ASQ Quality Press, 2007). This is a detailed encyclopedia and reference for the methods to identify constraints and resolve them, rich in examples. This book is a deeply revised version of the previous Breaking the constraints to world-leading performance.

Fedurko, Jelena: Mistakes and difficulties in working with TOC logical tools

After having used TOC tools (CRT, PRT, FRT and others) for some time there is more to learn in how to use these tools. Jelena Fedurko's book is a helpful guideline. (Also available as CD).

Most efforts in operational leadership are some kind of projects, so they suffer from the typical problems of not achieving the planned result and running both over time and cost budget. TOC based project management (CCPM or "critical chain") improves project performance significantly.

Operational leaders special challenge is to manage many projects in parallel. Gerry Kendall's books are guides to cope with these challenges:

Kendall, Gerry: Advanced project portfolio management

Gerry is a renowned practitioner and coach in this field; his books offer a good description of this approach.

For operational leaders of production units TOC is rich with insights, approaches and methods, which result in improving performance.

Cohen, Oded: Ever improve

Oded has life long experience in transforming production units to leading performance. His book based on that practical experience is a well-written guide to managing production the TOC way.

About HP

Packard, David: The HP Way, How Bill Hewlett and I built our company.

(Harper Business. 1995). A small MUST READ book. Packard lays out the foundations of HPs outstanding performance – technically and culturally.

Malone, Michael S.: Bill and Dave. How Hewlett and Packard built the world's greatest company.

(Penguin Books. 2007)

House, Charles H. and Price, Raymond L.: The HP Phenomenon.

(Stanford University Press. 2009)
Chuck House was a key person in HP, leading many breakthrough developments, and a vivid proponent of the HP Way. He shares many principles and practices that made HP masters of operational excellence.

About decision making

Kahneman, Daniel: Thinking, fast and slow.

(McMillan, 2011.) Kahnemann shows our limits as rational decision makers – but also offers ways out of the traps of purely intuitive decision-making. In our book we discuss only two of his key points, more reading recommended. Good to have pencil and paper ready to reflect what his views mean for us business people.

Watzlawik, Paul: How real is real?

(Vintage, 1977). A classic. How can we ever understand what REALLY goes on in our company?

Branka Zei-Pollermann, Unified Model of Cognition, Emotion and Action

A presentation at the University of Louvain, 2006. This paper gives a wider overview of how cognition (how we realize what there is), emotions and actions are related.

Index

A

Accountability
　Adjustment in quick reviews, 156
Accountable
　For speed of PEC cycle, 88
　Owner of necessary condition, 96
　RACI model, 96
Adjusting structure of operational plans, 135
Advantage of not planning, 55
Agenda
　Deep review, 157
　Operational planning workshop, 148
　Quick review, 156
Agile operational leadership, 21
　Deep reviews, 130
　Operational sprint, 23
Agile software development
　Defined, 21
Agility
　Defined, 171
Arthur, James L. (Jim), 152
Autopoiesis, 31

B

Bandle, Alain, 189
Bertallanffy, Ludwig von, 194
Bertallanfy, Ludwig von
　Book 'General system theory', 194
Bobst, Jean-Pascal, 189
BOEING
　Ecosystem for Dreamliner, 26
Bonaparte, Napoleon
　On checking for obstacles, 108
　On keeping promises, 119
Boyd, John, 85
　OODA loop, 24
　Presentations on OODA loop, 193
Branham, Leigh
　Book 'The 7 hidden reasons emploees leave', 177
Business ecosystem
　And critical success factors, 74
　Changing, 31
　Checking the whole for critical success factors, 76
　Defined, 26
　Example BOEING, 26
　Goals for elements, 42
Business system
　A social system, 32
　Autonomous, 31
　Autopoietic, 31
　Defined, 25
　Mapped in operational planning workshop, 150
　Self organizing, 31
　Self reproducing, 31
Business unit
　See company business unit, 67
BVI (brainstorm-vote-implement), 51

C

Cohen, Oded
　Book 'Ever improve', 195
Commitment
　As necessary condition, 37
　Building milestones, 114
　DoD milestones, 114
　Milestones, 114
　Phrased as DoD, 113
　Phrased to overcome obstacles, 115
　Single DoD, 113
　System state to be achieved, 112
　To resolve emotional obstacle, 113

Way around obstacle, 115
Worksheet, 116
Company business unit
   Cross functional, 41, 67
   Income generating, 41
   Matrix units, 41
   Three types, 41
Competitive battlefield, 81
Competitors
   As constraints, 84
   Battlefield, 81
   Competitors' plans, 89
   Creating contraints for CSFs, 81
   Key competitors, 89
   OODA loop in business competition, 88
   Speed, decisive for winning, 85
   Systems view, 81
Constraint
   Brought out by breakthrough goals, 43
   Caused by competitors, 84
   Data proof for causality, 53
   Defined, 29
   Exploiting, 174
   Finding, 136
   Managers, as, 172
   Not found intuitively, 53
   Of management capacity, 174
   Plan to resolve, 140
   Root cause of undesired effect, 29
   Speed of resolution as competitive element, 88
   Systemic, 66
   Two steps to find, 137
Contribution margin
   As single operational goal, 40
   Defined, 40
Critical chain, 195
Critical success factor
   At operational level, 73
   At strategic level, 73
   Changing over time, 74
   Defined, 36
   Different by business unit, 73
   Different by customer, 73
   For social dimension, 76
   Internal and external, 74
   Phrased as system state, 76
   Rules to set CSF right, 76
   WYSIATI trap, 76
Cross functional business units, 67
CRT. *See Current reality tree*
CSF. See critical success factor
Csikszentmihalyi, Mihaly
   Book 'Good business', 177, 193
Culture of high reliability, 169
Culture of operational excellence, 32
   Example HP Way, 166
Current reality tree
   In deep reviews, 136
   Step 1, Find causal clusters, 137
   Step 2, Compile CRT, 139

D

Daily stand up meeting, 21
Decisions
   Emotional, 105
   Rational, 105
Deep review
   Adjusting structure of operational plans, 135
   Agenda, 158
   Defined, 20
   Element of agile operational leadership, 24
   Excellence in operational leadership quadrant, 131
   Four situations, 130
   Got it wrong quadrant, 133
   Improving obligation management, 134
   Lucky win quadrant, 131
   Refining the operational plan, 135
   Wrong plan quadrant, 132
Definition of Done
   Defined, 69
   In operational leadership, 70
   Software trap, 71
DELTA T Cockpit, 183
   Ease of use, 187

Simplifies task of operational leadership, 185
Deming, William Edwards, 24
Dettmer, H. William, 3, 22, 194
  Book 'Breaking the constraints to world class performance', 137
  Book 'The logical thinking process', 136
  On overcoming obstacles, 115
  On team responsible for a goal, 46
Diaz, Manuel F., 104, 168
DoD. *See Definition of done*
Drucker, Peter
  Book 'The practice of management', 193
  On management creating constraints, 104

E

Ecosystem. *See business ecosystem*
Ellis-Jones, David, 189
Emotion, 176
Emotional abuse, 177
Emotional decisions, 105
Excellence in operational leadership
  Measuring in DELTA T Cockpit, 187
Exploiting a constraint, 174

F

Fedurko, Jelena
  Book ' Mistakes and difficulties in working with TOC logical tools', 194
Fontana, Mario, 189
FRT. *See Future reality tree*
Function performance goals
  Defined, 36
Future reality tree, 140
  In deep reviews, 136

G

Garelli, Stephane

Rule of survival in companies, 64
Goal
  And action, 34
  Defined - Systems view, 34
  For functions performance, 36
  In management value chain, 35
  Of a business - Eliyahu Goldratt, 39
  Operational business goal, 35
  Strategic, 37
Goal chart
  In execution of operational plan, 122
  Shared in meetings, 154
  Utmost simplicity, 45
Goldratt, Eliyahu, 194
  Book 'The goal', 194
  Five steps to address constraints, 174
  Goal of a business, 39
  POOGI cycle, 24
Gretzky, Wayne, 175

H

Hackborn, Richard A., 11
Halstead, Donald, 189
Hoshin planning
  One-page logic trees, 59
  Top-down deployment, 63
House, Charles H. (Chuck)
  Book 'The HP Phenomenon', 171, 195
HP
  10X project, 154
  As showcase of operational excellence, 17
  Business results, 18
  Competitive speed of developing products, 88
  Critical success factors for entering printer business, 75
  HP Way, 166

I

Injection, 140

Law of unintended consequences, 140
INSEAD, 14

J

Jumping to conclusions, 52

K

Kahnemann, Daniel, 49, 50
    Book 'Thinking, fast and slow', 196
Kano, Noriaki
    Recommending one-page plans, 58
Kemp, Owen, 189
Kendall, Gerry
    Book 'Advanced project portfolio management', 195
Key events schedule
    Defined, 151
Key leadership event
    Deep review, 157
    Meeting, 154
    Operational planning workshop, 145
    Quick review, 155
Klinkmueller, Johannes E., 189
Kober, Hanns-Per
    Example for going around obstacles, 115
Kotter, John P.
    On recognizing operational leadership as separate management discipline, 14

L

Law of unintended consequences, 140
Leader
    Added value, 143
Liebmann, Hans-Peter, 189
    On the need to lead business as value-adding system, 25

M

Madec, Michel, 59, 132
Malone, Michael s.
    Book 'Bill and Dave.', 166
    Book 'Bill and Dave', 195
Management value chain, 12
Matrix organization, 67
Maturana, Humberto R., 194
    On autopoietic systems, 31
MbO - Management by objectives, 62
Migy, Gabriel, 3, 189
Milestones
    For commitments, 114
Mintzberg, Henry
    Book 'The rise and fall of strategic planning', 23
    On top-down planning, 63
Monroe, Marylin
    On difficulty to be on time, 126
Moore, James F.
    On definition of business ecosystems, 26

N

Napoleon. *See Bonaparte*
Nawratil, Franz, 189
    On killing own products faster than competitors, 88
Necessary conditions
    Defined, 95
    Level of ownership, 97
    Sharing progress in meetings, 154
    Tracking execution, 124
    Worksheet, 99

O

Obligation
    Terms used in operational plans, 37
Obligations
    All confirmed, 119
    Personal obligation process, 127
Obligations pipeline

Defined, 134
Obstacles
   Checking the whole business system, 108
   Defined, 103
   Defined by System 1, 107
   Emotional, 104
   Emotional decisions, 105
   One obstacle per phrase, 108
   Physical, 104
OODA loop, 24
   Four phases, 86
   In business competition, 88
Operational business goals
   And balanced score card, 40
   Defined, 35
   For company units, 41
   For income generating business units, 42
   Incentive goals separate, 43
   Right content, 43
Operational excellence
   Defined, 13
   Management's view, 16
   Two views, 16
Operational goals
   Breakthrough goals, 43
   Hockey stick goals, 45
   Inflating, 43
   Milestones, 45
   Product rollovers, 46
   Right for leading execution, 45
   Seasonality, 46
   Single accountable owner, 46
Operational leaders
   Content experts, 172
Operational leadership
   Creates company success, 13
   Delegating
      don't even think of it, 174
   Four key events, 144
   Not recognized, 14
   Role in management value chain, 13
Operational performance
   Four quadrants, 130
   Two dimensions, 130

Operational plan
   As backlog of operational sprint, 24
   Autonomous for business units, 66
   Causal/logic tree, 57
   For cross functional business units, 67
   In matrix organizations, 67
   Not completed unless all obligations confirmed, 119
   One-page, 58
   Owning quality of, 152
   Systemic constraint, 66
   Two purposes, 56
Operational planning workshop
   Agenda, 148
   Don't rush, 153
   For multiple units, 146
   Goal charts, 149
   Light and full version, 147
   Need the full operational team, 152
   Preparation, 146
   System diagram, 150
Operational project, 26
Operational sprint
   Completed, 129
   Defined, 23
Operational team
   Accepted goal chart, 149
   Agree on business system, 150
   Defined, 61
   Surfing on one board, 122
Operationalization
   Defined, 68
Operationalize
   Commitments, 113
   Competitors' plans, 89
   Necessary conditions, 96
   Obstacles, 107
   Organization, 176

P

Packard, David W.
   Book 'How Bill Hewlett and I built our company', 175, 195
   On centralized management, 175

On the purpose of a business, 38
PEC cycle
   And OODA loop, 88
   Defined, 23
   Leading with four key events, 144
Personal obligation process, 127
Policy
   As obstacle, 104
POOGI cycle, 24
Prerequisite tree, 58
Priming, 51
Production management
   Book 'Ever improve', 195
Productivity
   As operational business goal, 40
Project management
   Book 'Advanced project portfolio management', 195

Q

Quadrant of operational performance, 130
Quick review
   Agenda, 156
   Defined, 20
   Element of agile operational leadership, 24

R

RACI model of roles in project management, 96
Rational decisions, 105
Reliability
   Lack of, main cause for operational failure, 126
   Why people break promises, 126
Rozwadowski, Tony, 189
Russell, William V. (Bill), 189
   On the added value of leaders, 143
   On the advantage of not planning, 55

S

S.R.N., 32, 48, 177
Scrum
   Daily stand up meeting, 21
   Sprint retrospective, 21
Sharing goals and plans, 170
Sherburne, Cary, 3
Shewhart, Walter A., 24
Six Sigma, 24
Slatford, Karen, 189
Soin, Sarv Singh, 3
   Book 'Total quality essentials', 173
   Book 'Winning with operational excellence', 193
   In God we trust, 49
   On 9 step business plan, 16
   On assessing operational competence, 160
Soto, Juan
   On limits of top-down planning, 63
Sprint retrospective, 21
Strategic goals
   Defined, 37
Sun Tzu
   On knowing the enemy, 81
   On ways to cope with competition, 98
Switzerland
   Multi-lingual keyboards, 29
System 1
   Defined, 50
   Jumping to conclusions, 52
   Priming, 51
   WYSIATI trap, 51
System 2
   Defined, 50
   In operational planning workshop, 147
System state
   Commitments, 113
Systemic constraint, 66
Systems view
   Competitors, 81
   Constraint, 29

T

TETRA PAK, 115
Theory of constraints
    Current reality tree, CRT, 136
    Future reality tree, 136
    Legat/Woehr book on sales leadership, 6
    Throughput, 40
Thing, Jens, 189
Throughput (T)
    TOC measure of sufficient income, 40
Tilman, H.W.
    Book 'Mount Everest 1938', 58
    On one-page plans, 58
Top-down planning
    Two assumptions, 63
Tracey, Nigel, 189

U

UDE. *See Undesired effect*
Undesired effect, 29, 138, 139, 140

V

Value-generating network, 38
Varela, Francisco J., 194
    On autopoietic systems, 31
Vision
    Information for critical success factors, 15

W

Watzlawik, Paul
    Book 'How real is real?', 196
    Book 'How real is real?', 51
Weiner, Georg
    On right business goals, 39
Woehr, William A., 3
Worksheet
    Commitments, 116
    Competitors' plans, 90
    Critical success factors, 77
    Necessary conditions, 99
    Obstacles, 108
WYSIATI, 51

Y

Young, John A.
    Example for leading key operational projects, 154

Z

Zei-Pollermann model, 113
Zei-Pollermann, Branka, 3
    On emotions at work, 176
    On ignoring emotional obstacles, 104
    Presentation 'Unified model of cognition, emotion and action', 196

Also by Dieter Legat

This book is about sales and selling management with a system's approach based on Goldratt's Theory of Constraints. Goldratt, Dettmer and many others have shown for some time that enterprises are limited or blocked in reaching success by their constraints. Bill Woehr and Dieter Legat show with this book that these constraints become visible when the sales system meets the customer. These constraints have become the question of survival.

When we applied TOC (theory of constraints) to our sales systems we were positively surprised to find that our enterprises are not victims of the "lousy economy" but of internal constraints, which we impose on ourselves. We cannot see the opportunities we actually face. We are victims of the "economy" and are forced to cut cost and down size our enterprises.

This book shows a way out. A "how to" book, which every top sales manager can use to lead his/her organization through the required transformation. To succeed in this transformation however, top sales managers must radically reshape the assumptions, which guide their decisions. They must change the whole value system of the sales organization. Without this change, the authors give few chances for enterprises to survive in the global economy.

As our teacher Dr. Deming once said, "survival is not mandatory" This book is provocative-a MUST for all top sales managers who want to "LEAD AND NOT FOLLOW".

Available at TOC Goldratt